Oxford Modern Britain   SERIES EDITOR: JOHN SCOTT

Age and Generation in Modern Britain

The *Oxford Modern Britain* series comprises authoritative introductory books on all aspects of the social structure of modern Britain. Lively and accessible, the books will be the first point of reference for anyone interested in the state of contemporary Britain. They will be invaluable to those taking courses in the social sciences.

ALSO PUBLISHED IN THIS SERIES

Race and Ethnicity in Modern Britain
David Mason

Religion in Modern Britain
Steve Bruce

Youth and Employment in Modern Britain
Kenneth Roberts

FORTHCOMING TITLES

Women and Work in Modern Britain
Rosemary Crompton

Kinship in Modern Britain
Graham Allan

Voting Behaviour in Modern Britain
Anthony Heath

Health and Healthcare in Modern Britain
Joan Busfield

Age and Generation
in Modern Britain

Jane Pilcher

OXFORD UNIVERSITY PRESS
1995

Oxford University Press, Walton Street, Oxford OX2 6DP

Oxford New York
Athens Auckland Bangkok Bombay
Calcutta Cape Town Dar es Salaam Delhi
Florence Hong Kong Istanbul Karachi
Kuala Lumpur Madras Madrid Melbourne
Mexico City Nairobi Paris Singapore
Taipei Tokyo Toronto
and associated companies in
Berlin Ibadan

Oxford is a trade mark of Oxford University Press

Published in the United States
by Oxford University Press Inc., New York

British Library Cataloguing in Publication Data
Data available

Library of Congress Cataloging in Publication Data
Data available
ISBN 0-19-827961-2
ISBN 0-19-827962-0 (Pbk.)

1 3 5 7 9 10 8 6 4 2

Typeset by Hope Services (Abingdon) Ltd.
Printed in Great Britain
on acid-free paper by
Biddles Ltd.,
Guildford & King's Lynn

To my Great Auntie, May Teal (1903–88), and to my Grandparents,
both living and departed.

Foreword

The Oxford Modern Britain series is designed to fill a major gap in the available sociological sources on the contemporary world. Each book will provide a comprehensive and authoritative overview of major issues for students at all levels. They are written by acknowledged experts in their fields, and should be standard sources for many years to come.

Each book focuses on contemporary Britain, but the relevant historical background is always included, and a comparative context is provided. No society can be studied in isolation from other societies and the globalized context of the contemporary world, but a detailed understanding of a particular society can both broaden and deepen sociological understanding. These books will be exemplars of empirical study and theoretical understanding.

Books in the series are intended to present information and ideas in a lively and accessible way. They will meet a real need for source books in a wide range of specialized courses, in 'Modern Britain' and 'Comparative Sociology' courses, and in integrated introductory courses. They have been written with the newcomer and general reader in mind, and they meet the genuine need in the informed public for accurate and up-to-date discussion and sources.

John Scott
Series Editor

Acknowledgements

Formal acknowledgements are due to: Posy Simmonds for permission to reproduce her cartoon; Age Concern for permission to reproduce their campaign poster; Policy Studies Institute for permission to reproduce material used in Chapter Three; Office of Population Censuses and Surveys for material used in Chapter One. In addition, I would like to thank: John Scott for his advice and constructive criticism; Dianne Orme, Jan Stephens, and Pat Mumby for their help in typing the manuscript; and, finally, love and thanks to Eddie May for his encouragement and support.

Contents

List of Figures and Tables

Figures

Tables

Concepts and Measurement

Writing in 1986, Finch described the sociology of age as 'relatively uncharted territory' (Finch 1986: 12). Since then, increasing attention has been paid by sociologists to the importance of age and there is now a significant body of literature that covers the social aspects of the human ageing process. This book draws upon the available body of evidence about age and generation in modern Britain. It aims to illustrate the various ways in which age acts to fundamentally shape peoples' identities, experiences, and opportunities. Evidence is presented which shows that, like social class, ethnicity, and gender, age is a social category through which people define and identify individuals and groups within society. Age is both an important part of how we see ourselves and how others see us. It is shown that age acts as an important basis for the distribution of social prestige and status within modern Britain. Access to power, material resources, and citizenship rights are also shown to be structured by age.

This chapter introduces the reader to thinking about age from a sociological perspective and addresses the question 'What is age?' by considering the key ageing processes. Demographic data is presented which provides an age profile of modern Britain. Comparisons are drawn historically and between various subgroups of the population, including women and men, and between ethnic groups.

Sociology and Age

One of the most distinctive contributions of sociology as a discipline has been to show that aspects of human lives and behaviour once thought to be determined solely by nature or biology are, in fact, heavily influenced by the particular *social* environment in which people live. Differences between men and women and between various 'races' are now understood to be socially constructed and perpetuated, rather than biologically determined. It is in recognition of this changed understanding about the primary source of differences between women and men that we now speak of 'gender' rather than of 'sex' differences. Similarly, we speak of 'ethnic groups' and of 'ethnicity', rather than of 'racial groups' and of 'races', in recognition of the fact that 'differences' between groups in society have more to do with *culture* than with biology.

In the cases of gender and ethnicity, then, social and cultural factors are fully recognized and are accorded priority in any explanation of differences between individuals and groups within society. In the case of age, however, full recognition of the role played by social and cultural factors in shaping the ways in which human beings grow up and grow old is a fairly recent development. Of course, sociologists accept that there are physiological differences between persons of different ages, in the same way that they accept that there are visible differences in the bodies of women and men and of, say, skin colour between different peoples of the world. However, in each case, it is not the physiological differences that primarily interest sociologists but the ways in which various societies at various times interpret, understand, and attach significance to such differences. This is an important theme that runs throughout the book. Here, two brief examples are given to illustrate the different interpretations placed upon age according to time and place.

In contemporary British society, children's lives are organized in a radically different manner from those of adults. Up until age 16 or so, children's lives are controlled and regulated to such an extent that we can say there is an institutionalized separation of the world of children from that of adults. This way of organizing adult–child relations, as Chapter Three explains, is seen as natural and is largely taken for granted, as are the numerical markers of childhood. However, evidence shows that in earlier periods of history, this separation of the worlds of children and adults was much less marked and, indeed, much shorter. Aries (1962) has shown how, in medieval times, 'children' aged over 5 were regarded as small adults and were integrated into the adult world.

Old age provides a second example of the way in which the physiological aspects of growing older are variously interpreted by different cultures around the world. In British society, older people are encouraged to conceal grey hair, wrinkles, and other signs of ageing. Yet, among the Venda-speaking people of southern Africa, such physical indicators of old age are welcomed as a sign of nearer contact with the world of the spirits (Blacking 1990, cited in Hockey and James 1993).

If we look, then, at different cultures around the world or at any one society over its history, we can see that whilst the physiological aspects of growing up and growing older are more or less universal, the ways in which the ageing process is understood varies over time and place. The sociological perspective on age is that the significance of age is *socially constructed*. Rather than being a natural consequence of their age, the prohibition of children from formal employment and the dependency of older retired people on income from pensions, for example, are the direct outcomes of social and cultural practices, including political and economic policies. In other words, chronological age on its own is not deterministic; it is subject to social and cultural intervention, at different times and different places.

What is 'Age'?

In Western cultures, a person's age is counted on a chronological, numerical basis, beginning from year of birth to the current point of reference, or in the case of death, until the year in which death occurred. Thus, a person born in 1953 and alive in 1994 would be 41 years old. A person born in 1920 and who died in 1982 would have been 62 years old. In Western societies, a person's chronological age, calculated on this precise basis, is extremely important. It is used to prohibit, compel, or permit individuals to participate in certain activities, according to their year of birth. In other cultural traditions, particularly pre-industrial societies, chronological age is neither recognized nor accorded such great significance. As Fortes (1984) explains, the concept of a date, by numbering a year, is not always found in the traditional cultures of Africa or other continents. This is not to say that such societies lack a calendar but rather that the passing of time may be measured by points of reference to important events and occurrences within the culture's structure and ongoing routines. Examples here might be severe climatic events, like a typhoon, or maturational events, like puberty. In Western societies, the dating system and the numerical counting of age on which it is based, depend upon literacy, numeracy, and the techniques of science (Fortes 1984), and should be recognized as merely one way of conceptualizing time and of measuring age. In itself, then, counting age by reference to a numerical dating system is a social construction. It is a practice linked to specific conceptions of clock and calendar time in Western societies, which came to be of increasing importance with the development of capitalism (Thompson 1967).

Although recognizing that it is a social construction, sociologists are less interested in chronological or numerical age than in what this measurement of age tells them about an individual. Chronological age, although it is not a perfect indicator, is useful for locating an individual within the key aspects of the ageing process.

Physiological age

As individuals age in chronological terms, they also age in biological or physiological terms. Human ageing unavoidably entails a series of physical transformations over time. Babies grow and develop into children. Children, via puberty, develop into persons capable of sexual reproduction. Later in the human life span, the capacity to sexually reproduce declines and, especially for women, is ultimately lost. Biological ageing also involves growing and losing different types of teeth, developing secondary sexual characteristics (such as body hair), losing elasticity of skin tone, developing wrinkles and grey hair, and a reduction of physical capacities. In these various ways, age has a biological reality which, although increasingly subject to medical or related technological interventions, remains a universal aspect of human life with a progressive dynamic of its own, largely beyond human control.

The life course

Anthropological and sociological evidence shows that societies tend to group persons together on the basis of their similar age, and by the typical behaviour patterns and social roles culturally expected to be associated with that age. Around the world, the human span of life from birth to death is variously divided into *stages*, where individuals, within a range of ages, may be grouped together on the basis of their similar roles and status, relative to persons at earlier, or later, stages. Age may, therefore, be used as an index to locate an individual's likely position in the 'life course', in a socially defined 'timetable' of behaviours deemed as appropriate for particular life stages within any one society. This way of thinking about growing up and growing old is discussed in more detail in Chapter Two. The notion of the life course has also proved to be a useful way of ordering the contents of this book. Evidence on childhood is discussed first (Chapter Three), followed by youth (Chapter Four), adulthood and middle age (Chapter Five), and then later life and old age (Chapter Six).

Cohort membership

Age is counted, in Western cultures at least, in terms of calendar time. A person of a particular numerical age is, correspondingly, also a person who has lived through a particular *historical* period. As a consequence, individuals are exposed to certain experiences, opportunities, and crises and are excluded from others. For example, a 27-year-old man in 1994 was not born and could not have experienced the Second World War (1939–45). Similarly, a woman who lived between 1850 and 1915 could never have voted in a general election, because women did not gain the vote until 1918. A man born in 1926 could leave school at 14, but a boy born in 1970 had to remain at school until at least age 16. In these various ways, then, the period of history through which individuals live acts to shape the range and possibilities of experience. This cohort membership aspect of the ageing process in explored further in Chapter Two and again in Chapter Eight.

Age, then, has three main dimensions of interest to sociologists. First, age and ageing have a biological or physiological dimension, so that over time, the appearance and capabilities of our physical bodies change quite dramatically. Second, as human beings, we live in societies, each with culturally defined expectations of how persons of particular ages are supposed to behave. As a person grows older, she or he is generally expected to progress through a series of statuses, positions, and relationships according to that culture's definitions and markers, and to interpretations placed upon the significance of indicators of physiological age, such as height or wrinkles. Third, the ageing of an individual, in both physiological and social-cultural terms, always takes place within a particular period of history, marked in its extreme from year of birth (say, 1905) to year of death (say, 1988). By virtue of this unavoidable fact, people's experiences are set or constrained by their location in historical time. Age must be understood as a simultaneous combination of these interrelated processes: of biological or physiological ageing; of social or cultural ageing; both of which take place within particular historical contexts. The importance of each dimension of ageing must be recognized, along with the relationships between them.

From a sociological viewpoint, then, age is rather a complex phenomenon. A further source of complexity is its transience as a social category (Babad, Birnbaum, and Benne 1983). Every person ages, in both physiological and social terms. Moreover, these processes take place in societies where historical time marches on relentlessly. Other dimensions of social selves, such as 'race', sex, or even social class, remain much more constant throughout an individual's life. Yet there is a real sense in which age as a social category remains constant, in that the entire membership of a cohort moves *together*, from one age to another. In other words, cohort members *grow up and grow old together*. The transient nature of age as a social category is therefore accompanied by a constancy of age group membership throughout the span of life (Babad, Birnbaum, and Benne 1983: 194).

In any discussion of age and generation, it is important to clarify matters of terminology. In particular, there is scope for confusion between 'cohort' and 'generation'. *Cohort* is a demographic term in origin. It is used to refer to a defined population who experience the same significant event at, or within, a given period of calendar time. Events such as birth, leaving school, or the Second World War would be examples of such significant events. As Finch (1986) points out, though, the potential of cohort in relation to age is greatest where a cohort is comprised of people born in the same year (or other given time interval) who then age *together*. Such a cohort would then leave school, experience the Second World War, and enter retirement, say, at around the same chronological age.

Generation is a structural term in kinship studies denoting the parent–child relationship (Glenn 1977). In everyday language, however, generation acts as a folk model conceptualization of what are, properly, cohort processes, as in 'the sixties generation'. This synonymous use of 'generation' for 'cohort' is also evident in the writings of some sociologists, including those of an important theorist, Karl Mannheim. Yet, it is important to maintain a conceptual distinction between kinship relationships and cohort processes. Using the same term to refer to both types of age relationships is obviously unwise and leads to much confusion. In this book, the term *generation* is only used when reference is made to kinship relationships within families. Thus *intergenerational relationships* refers to relationships between parents, children, and grandparents.

The Age Structure of the British Population: Past, Present, and Future

As later chapters will show, different age groups make different demands on society and contribute in different ways to its activities. Changes in the age composition of the population can, therefore, have important consequences for the distribution of power and resources between different age groups within society. Changes in the age structure can also affect relationships between age groups within families, this being the sense for which the phrase 'intergenerational relations' should properly be reserved.

The relative size of age groups within a population at any one point in time is the result of complex and long-term interactions between fertility rates, mortality rates, and levels of migration. For example, relatively low levels of birth in any one period would mean a relatively smaller proportion of a particular age group in the future. Similarly, an older age group may have had its numbers depleted, through high rates of mortality amongst its young men during wartime, or through its members having emigrated when younger.

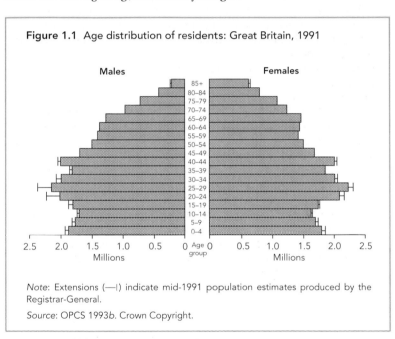

Figure 1.1 Age distribution of residents: Great Britain, 1991

Note: Extensions (—|) indicate mid-1991 population estimates produced by the Registrar-General.

Source: OPCS 1993b. Crown Copyright.

The age structure of British society in 1991 is shown in Figure 1.1. Its shape resembles that of a beehive (Coleman and Salt 1992). There are two noticeable peaks, one for people in their mid-forties and one for people in their late twenties. Both of these peaks are the consequences of 'baby booms': the first is a reflection of the high birth-rates which followed the end of the Second World War, whilst the second reflects the high birth-rates of the 1960s. As these large cohorts have grown up, they have placed particular strains on society in terms of their use of state services and resources; for example, in their need for schooling and for employment. Issues arising from the size of cohorts are discussed in Chapter Eight, which also considers the contributions cohorts can make to society via their role in social and cultural change. The challenges for society that can accompany large cohorts as they become aged, and hence more reliant on pensions and other forms of welfare services, are considered in Chapter Seven. One aspect of this challenge is indicated by the low number of births in the middle and the late 1970s, which was preceded by the higher birth-rate of the earlier decades (Figure 1.1). During their working lives, the smaller cohort of the 1970s will be supporting a large cohort of retired persons. This scenario, of a small age group of working age supporting a larger proportion of dependent aged persons, has been described as 'the demographic time bomb' and is discussed further in Chapter Seven. The implications of changes in the age structure for intergenerational relationships within families are also considered, including in terms of grandparent–grandchild relations.

The age structure of Britain in 1991 differs from the age structure at earlier periods in history. Figure 1.2 shows the distribution of the population by age for the period 1871 to 1971. In the late nineteenth century, the shape of the population structure was that of a pyramid, with a large proportion of younger people at the base and a small proportion of older people toward the top. As the twentieth century has progressed, the age composition of the population has changed quite dramatically and so the shape has gradually transformed, from a pyramid to a beehive. During this period, there has been an expansion in the proportions of middle-aged and older people and a reduction in the proportion of younger people. This change is due primarily to lower fertility rates in recent decades. As a consequence, Britain is described as having undergone an 'ageing of the population'. For example, the median average age of the population in 1901 was 24, whilst in 1931 it was 30.3. In 1981, it was calculated to have risen to 34.7 (Johnson and Falkingham 1992: 19).

Into the Twenty-First Century

What of the age structure of the British population in the future? Up until the year 2001, projections as to the age composition of the population can be made fairly accurately, since most people who will be alive

Figure 1.2 Age structure of England and Wales in five-year age groups, 1871–1971

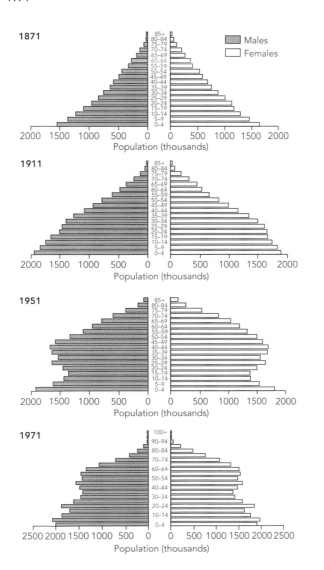

Source: Coleman and Salt 1992.

then are already born. However, after the year 2001, population projections are far less predictable (Johnson and Falkingham 1992: 42). Keeping this in mind, the following main changes in the age structure of the population of England and Wales (which comprises 88 per cent of the population of the United Kingdom) have been predicted by the Office of Population Censuses and Surveys (OPCS). First, the number of children under 16 is projected to rise by about 5 per cent between 1992 and 2002, then to fall slowly until 2020 and then to change little during the 2020s. Second, the population of working age (males aged 16–64 and females aged 16–59) is projected to grow by about 6 per cent to a peak of 33.2 million in 2011, and then fall by over 5 per cent over the following twenty years. The number of adults under 30 is projected to fall rapidly for the rest of the century and not to regain its present level within the next forty years. Third, the number of people over the present pensionable age (65 for men, 60 for women) is projected to increase by just over 2 per cent between 1992 and 2001, from 9.4 million to 9.6 million. It is then set to rise more quickly, to reach 14.8 million in 2032. This represents an increase of 50 per cent in just over 30 years (OPCS 1994a). The implications of this increase in terms of pressures on society's economic and welfare resources and for interage group relations are examined in Chapter Seven.

Overall, then, the established twentieth century trend of an ageing population is set to continue through to the twenty-first century. Over the period 1992 to 2032, while the total population of England and Wales is projected to rise by 8 per cent, the population aged 45–59 is projected to rise by 11 per cent and that aged 60–74 is projected to rise by 49 per cent. The proportions of people aged 75–84 and 85 and over are predicted to rise by 51 per cent and 126 per cent respectively (OPCS 1994a). These projected changes in the age structure of the population are largely the result of past fluctuations in the numbers of births, although improved mortality rates are also important. In fact, longevity at older ages can contribute significantly to the ageing of the elderly population itself (Johnson and Falkingham 1992: 21).

Variations in the Age Structure

The distribution of the population by age within the British population varies by a number of factors, including region and geographical location, gender, and ethnicity.

Region and geographical location

Whilst the age structure of the United Kingdom as whole is beehive in shape (Figure 1.1), the shape of the age structure in Northern Ireland is rather different. It resembles a pyramid rather than a beehive and is therefore more like the structure that was characteristic of Britain in the late nineteenth and early twentieth century (Figure 1.2). Compared to Britain as a whole, Northern Ireland has comparatively high rates of fertility, which gives its population structure a much broader base of young people (Coleman and Salt 1992).

Certain geographical locations within Britain also have distinctive age structures, due to the age-selective nature of the migration process (Coleman and Salt 1992). As Figure 1.3 shows, the elderly tend to be peripherally located, especially in the coastal areas, as a consequence of retirement migration. Meanwhile, there is a significant concentration of 25–44-year-olds to the north and west of London due to its vibrancy as an economic region, making it attractive to people of working age (Figure 1.4).

Ethnicity

The age structure of the British population varies by ethnic group. Figure 1.5 shows that the ethnic minority population is younger than the majority white population, with fewer being over pensionable age. This is a reflection of the history of immigration to Britain, particularly in the 1950s and 1960s. A third of the ethnic minority population is under age 16, compared with under one-fifth of the population in the white group. In contrast, only 3 per cent of the ethnic minority population are aged 65 and over, compared with 17 per cent of the population in the white group (OPCS 1993*a*). The great majority (80 per cent) of the ethnic minority population aged under 25 were born in the United Kingdom, compared with 15 per cent of those aged 25 and over (OPCS 1994*b*).

There are differences of age structure between the various ethnic minority groups, which reflect the differing patterns of immigration to Britain. Although having a younger age structure than the white population, long-established ethnic minority groups, like the Black Caribbeans, have an older age structure than more recently arrived groups, such as those of Bangladeshi and Pakistani origin. For example, 21 per cent of the white population are in the 0–15 age group, compared with 25 per cent of the Black Caribbean and 47 per cent of the Pakistani/Bangladeshi population. Only 2 per cent of the population of

Figure 1.3 Percentage of residents aged 60 and over, Great Britain, 1991

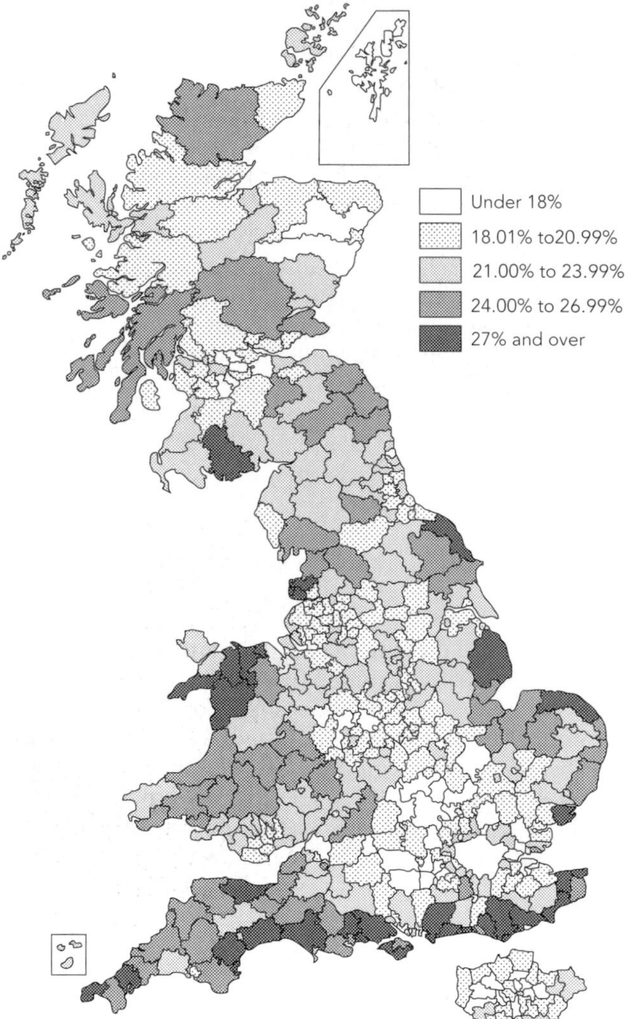

Legend:
- Under 18%
- 18.01% to 20.99%
- 21.00% to 23.99%
- 24.00% to 26.99%
- 27% and over

Source: OPCS 1993c. Crown Copyright.

Figure 1.4 Age structure by local labour market areas, 25–44-year-olds as percentage of total, 1981

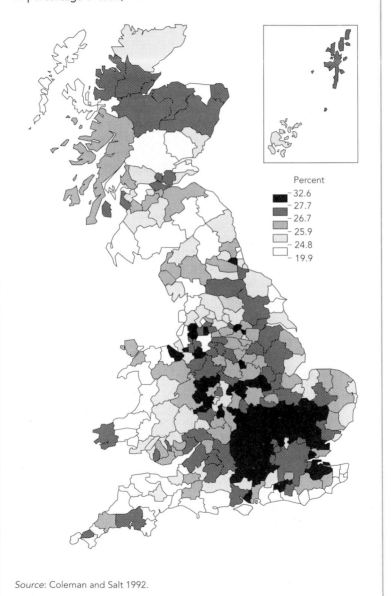

Percent
- 32.6
- 27.7
- 26.7
- 25.9
- 24.8
- 19.9

Source: Coleman and Salt 1992.

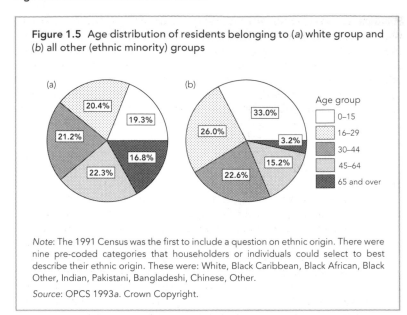

Figure 1.5 Age distribution of residents belonging to (a) white group and (b) all other (ethnic minority) groups

Age group
- 0–15
- 16–29
- 30–44
- 45–64
- 65 and over

Note: The 1991 Census was the first to include a question on ethnic origin. There were nine pre-coded categories that householders or individuals could select to best describe their ethnic origin. These were: White, Black Caribbean, Black African, Black Other, Indian, Pakistani, Bangladeshi, Chinese, Other.

Source: OPCS 1993a. Crown Copyright.

Pakistani origin are aged 65 and over, compared with around 23 per cent of both the white and Black Caribbean populations (OPCS 1994b).

Gender

Women make up a slightly greater proportion of the population than men, at around 52 per cent. The differences in the age distribution of women and men, however, only become significant in the latter half of the life course. In 1992, the ratio of men to women in the 60–4 age group was 50:50. However, at ages 65–9, there were 47 males to 53 females, whilst at age 70–4 the ratio was 44:56. At age 75 and over, the ratio of males to females decreased still further to 38:62 (OPCS 1994b). Women have greater life expectancies than men, so that amongst the elderly and the very elderly, they significantly outnumber men. Arber and Ginn (1991) have referred to this process as the 'feminization of later life'. The social and economic position of old people in modern British society is the focus of Chapter Six, where particular attention is paid to the experiences of old women.

This chapter has argued that what we refer to as 'age' is a product of three interrelated processes: of physiology, of stage in life course, and of location in historical time, via cohort membership. It has suggested that interpretations and understandings of age vary over time and place and this is a theme that will feature throughout the book. The demographic data have shown that the population of modern Britain is comprised of age groups of different sizes, which leads to its beehive shape. Historical comparisons have been made which reveal that the relative sizes of age groups have changed over the course of the twentieth century. Within the population of contemporary Britain, the distribution of the population by age has been shown to be affected by regional and geographical location, by gender and by ethnicity.

The following chapters concentrate on illuminating the role age (or rather, the interpretations placed upon its *significance*) plays in shaping experiences and structuring opportunities throughout the life course. Chapters Three to Six review evidence on age in modern Britain across the main stages of the life course, that is, childhood, youth, adulthood, and old age. At each stage of the life course, interrelations between the key aspects of the ageing process are considered and attention is paid to the ways in which age, cohort, and generation are mediated by gender, ethnicity, and social class. Chapter Seven focuses on the issue of interage group relationships, both within families and between age groupings within wider society. Chapter Eight is concerned with the importance of cohort membership and the ways in which it acts to shape identities, experiences, and opportunities. The concluding chapter locates the recent upsurge of interest in age in the context of demographic trends, technological interventions in physiological ageing processes, and debates about 'post-modernity'. In order that these chapters are grounded theoretically, Chapter Two provides an account of the main theoretical approaches taken in the sociology of age, including the cohort or social generational perspective of Mannheim, and the life course approach, advocated by Hareven, amongst others.

Further Reading

Finch (1986) is a useful introductory read to the importance of age as a key variable in sociological investigation. Babad, Birnbaum, and Benne (1983) pay attention to the relations between age and ethnicity and age and gender, as well as discussing interage group conflict and the 'generation gap'. Coleman and Salt (1992) provide a comprehensive account of trends in the British population.

Chapter Two

Social Theory and Age

This chapter reviews the ways in which sociologists have tried to explain the social significance of age. There are a number of preliminary remarks that need to be made, though, about the ways in which sociological theory has been applied to the study of age and age group relations. First, much of the research on age and age groups, broadly defined, has been undertaken by those whose primary interest lies elsewhere. For example, research on children has been conducted by sociologists of education, or of the family. Similarly, research on youth has been undertaken by sociologists of popular culture, or of employment and the labour market. Consequently, these writers have been concerned with contributing to the development of theory in their fields of primary interest, rather than in the field of age. Secondly, where particular theories about the social significance of age have been a primary concern, there has been a tendency to focus on one discrete stage of the life course and not to apply that theory to any other stages or to the life course as a whole. So, for example, the political economy perspective (discussed below) has been explicitly applied to the study of old age but less explicitly to the study of childhood. Thirdly, different sociological theories of age are concerned with differing aspects of the social significance of age and of interage group relations. Some are concerned with the individual's adjustment to growing older, others are concerned more with cohort processes, and still others are concerned with the relative distribution of status and material disadvantage between age groups. Taken together, these features mean that theorizing on age, generation, and cohort is underdeveloped and limited, in that there is no one overarching theory. Rather, there is a somewhat heterogeneous bundle of theories, each with a variety of concerns, strengths, and weaknesses.

This chapter introduces five theoretical perspectives on age and interage group relations which have, directly or indirectly, influenced how and what has been researched on age in modern Britain. These are:

the life course approach, cohort and social generation theory, functionalist perspectives, political economy, and interpretivist perspectives. The life course perspective is discussed in particular detail, since it provides an important framework for the book as a whole. Other theories are more briefly described and assessed. A fuller discussion of these takes place, where this is appropriate, in subsequent relevant chapters.

The categorization of the theories in the ways listed above, although based on real and substantive differences, is a somewhat artificial exercise, having benefits in terms of being able to clearly set them apart for purposes of review. In any empirical study of age or of age group relations, a variety of theoretical perspectives may in practice be employed, although, often, precisely which perspectives are employed may remain largely implicit (Fennell, Phillipson, and Evers 1988). A tendency to employ a range of theoretical perspectives may, in any case, be regarded as a necessary component of research on age, given its complexity as a sociological phenomenon.

For sociologists, ageing, the process of growing up and growing old, is socially constructed. In other words, sociologists argue that, whilst the physiological aspects of growing up and growing older are both universal and natural, the ways of understanding the ageing process are neither of these. Their concern is to explore the ways in which physiological processes of ageing are 'conceived and articulated in particular societies into culturally specific sets of ideas and philosophies, attitudes and practices' (Prout and James 1990: 1). This understanding of the centrality of cultural and historical *context* is, however, a recently articulated one. It is linked to the development of the life course perspective. Earlier theorizing on the nature of age and interage group relationships, particularly that which was conducted in the functionalist tradition, had rather different emphases, as we shall see.

The Life Course Perspective

The life course perspective is more of a way of conceptualizing the human span of life than an explanatory theory. None the less, it has become increasingly influential as a way of approaching the sociological study of age. The characteristics of the life course approach are best illustrated by comparing it with a previously dominant conceptualization of the span of human life: the *life cycle*. The concept of the life cycle describes the developmental stages that individuals undergo over time.

As they grow older, individuals progressively develop in physical, psychological, and social terms and so move, in sequence, through a fixed number of stages of the life cycle: infancy, childhood, youth, adulthood, and old age. As a concept, the life cycle has roots in the disciplines of biology and developmental psychology. This is the source of many of its weaknesses, from the viewpoint of sociology, because of its failure to take full account of *social* contexts.

The main weaknesses of the life cycle concept are argued to lie in its universalistic, deterministic, asocial, and ahistorical tendencies. As a cross-cultural survey by Ikels and colleagues (1992) illustrates, defining human life in terms of a fixed set of stages is very problematical because the number of different stages which are recognized varies greatly between cultures. Moreover, with average life expectancies ranging from the mid-thirties in, say, Afghanistan, to the high seventies in Britain, it cannot be assumed that 'stages' will be linked to chronological age or be experienced in universal ways (Monk and Katz 1993). It is difficult, then, to conceptualize the progression from birth to death without fully taking into account the cultural and historical *context* of that progression. For this reason the life cycle is an unsatisfactory conceptualization of the ways in which the individual progresses through the human span of life. It, nevertheless, has continuing currency as a folk model conceptualization of the 'cycle of life' (Bellaby 1987); for example, in the use of the language and imagery of childhood to describe the predicament of elderly people (Hockey and James 1993). This particular practice has a long history, as the quotation from Shakespeare indicates (see box opposite). Some social scientists also find continuing value in aspects of the life cycle conceptualization (e.g. Murphy 1987), including in the sense of individuals' 'recycling' their lives, through beginning new careers or new families (Monk and Katz 1993).

The acknowledged deficiencies of the life cycle concept have led it to be superseded by the alternative and now more highly favoured concept of the *life course*. Allatt and Keil argue that the contrast between the two concepts is one of a 'biological and social inevitability, irrespective of individual differences' (the life cycle), against one which allows for the 'interaction of the individual with social structures which are subject to historical change' (the life course) (1987: 1).

The concept of the life course is most closely associated with the American academic, Tamara Hareven. She summarizes its main characteristics as follows.

The life course approach provides a way of examining individual as well as collective development under changing historical conditions. It shifts the focus of

SHAKESPEARE'S SEVEN AGES

All the world's a stage
And all the men and women merely players;
They have their exits and their entrances;
And one man in his time plays many parts,
His acts being seven ages. At first the infant,
Mewling and puking in the nurse's arms;
Then the whining schoolboy, with his satchel
And shining morning face, creeping like snail
Unwillingly to school. And then the lover,
Sighing like furnace, with a woeful ballad
Made to his mistress' eyebrow. Then a soldier,
Full of strange oaths, and bearded like the pard,
Jealous in honour, sudden and quick in quarrel,
Seeking the bubble reputation
Even in the cannon's mouth. And then the justice,
In fair round belly with good capon lin'd,
With eyes severe and beard of formal cut,
Full of wise saws and modern instances;
And so he plays his part. The sixth age shifts
Into the lean and slipper'd pantaloon,
With spectacles on nose and pouch on side;
His youthful hose, well sav'd, a world too wide
For his shrunk shank; and his big manly voice,
Turning again toward childish treble, pipes
And whistles in his sound. Last scene of all,
That ends this strange eventful history,
Is second childishness and mere oblivion;
Sans teeth, sans eyes, sans taste, sans everything.

From Shakespeare's *As You Like It*

study of human development away from stages and ages to transitions and the timing of life events. Rather than focusing on stages of the life cycle, the life course approach is concerned with how individuals and families made their transitions into those different stages. Rather than viewing any one stage of life, such as childhood, youth, and old age, or any age group, in isolation, it is concerned with an understanding of the place of that stage in an entire life continuum. (Hareven 1982*a*: xiii)

It is clear from Hareven's description of the life course approach that it is a more fully sociological conceptual tool than that of the life cycle. Unlike the static, ages and stages, pre-ordered qualities suggested by the life cycle, the life course allows for flexibility and variation in stages reached, their timing and sequencing. The notion of *transition* is central to the life course approach, as is the processual nature of the routes or pathways that individuals make through their lives. Early transitions are seen to have consequences for the ways in which later ones are experienced, so that the birth to death passage is understood as comprising a set of interrelated events with cumulative outcomes. This issue is explored further in Chapter Six, where the greater material disadvantage experienced by women in old age, compared with men, is explained as a consequence of their *earlier* life histories.

Context is central to the conceptualization of the human life span as a life course, in the sense of social structural contexts as well as historical contexts. The life course approach allows us to see that 'ages and stages', and transitions between them, have culturally determined institutional bases, which may vary by historical context. Some writers have suggested that the life course is best viewed as a social institution in its own right, and one which is interconnected with other parts of the social structure, especially those of employment, families, and households (Kohli 1986; Featherstone and Hepworth 1989). Certainly, the life course approach is sensitive to the ways in which such institutions act to structure stages and transitions throughout an individual's life. It also, though, allows for individuals negotiating their way through the various structuring institutions (Jones and Wallace 1992). Seeing life courses as having culturally determined institutional bases explains the cross-cultural variation in 'ages and stages', as documented by Ikels *et al.* (1992). It also makes it possible to demonstrate the ways in which the life course changes, alongside changes in *other* societal institutions (Featherstone and Hepworth 1989).

Historical context (or time) is evidently crucial in understanding the experience of individuals as they grow up and grow older. The concept of time is central to the life course approach in other ways too. Hareven (1982b) distinguishes between different 'levels' of time which she sees as crucial to the interpretation and understanding of the life courses of individuals. These levels of time include 'family time', 'individual time', and 'historical time'. *Family time* refers to the timing of life course events, such as marriage or birth of a child, which involve the transition of individuals into different family roles (spouse, parent, sibling) as the family moves through its own life. *Individual time* is closely synchronized with family time, because most individual life transitions are interrelated with collective family transitions. Finally, *historical time* refers to the overall social and economic, institutional and cultural changes in the wider society, including demographic changes, economic constraints, and legal changes. According to Hareven, an understanding of the synchronization of the different levels of time is essential to the investigation of the relationship between individual lives and the larger process of social change. From the life course perspective, the most crucial aspect of timing is the point of intersection between an individual's (or a family's) life and historical forces (1982b: 7), Hareven further emphasizes the importance of historical time by specifying that cohort processes (the differences between cohorts arising from their location in historical time) are an essential aspect of the life course approach. Those theoretical perspectives which focus on the cohort aspect of the ageing process are discussed in the following section.

As a way of conceptualizing and analysing an individual's progression from birth to death, the life course perspective has few critics. It has been praised as an 'indispensable practical tool' (Harris 1987: 28) and a 'rich source of ideas and analytical principles' (Finch 1987: 168). The value of the life course perspective, most commentators agree, lies in the way it encapsulates the project of sociology as a discipline: that is, 'to grasp history and biography and the relations between the two within society' (Mills 1970: 12). Some criticisms, though, have been made against the generalized nature of the life course approach. For example, Murphy (1987) points out that there are few clear guide-lines for analysis, other than that no potentially important factor be ignored. For Jones and Wallace (1992), the generalized approach of the life course may lead attention to be overly focused on individuals rather than social groups. They suggest that some examples of the life course perspective have, as a consequence, lost sight of structural inequalities and the continuities of social reproduction.

Despite these criticisms, the life course is widely acknowledged as a more sensitive, flexible, and complex conceptualization of the process of growing up and growing old than that of the life cycle. The life course perspective has considerable value for the sociological study of age and interage group relationships, particularly arising from the theme of transition and the centrality of cultural and historical contexts. Transitions, or passages through various roles, relationships, statuses, institutions, and such like, as we grow up and older, involve transformations of identities and influence access to power and resources within society. Such transitions and transformations necessarily take place within cultural and historical contexts. To quote Riley (1984: 8), 'people do not grow up and grow old in laboratories'. In other words, ageing as a social phenomenon can only be fully understood through contextualizing physiological ageing within cultural and historical *contexts*. The life course approach provides a way of conceptualizing an individual's progression through life which is sensitive to the dynamic and cumulative nature of the ageing process, and its embedding in cultural and historical contexts. As such, the life course approach has become increasingly influential as a way of studying the social significance of age, as later chapters will illustrate.

Cohort and Social Generation Theory

Sociologically, the concept of cohort is a way of contextualizing the lives of individuals; first, within the specific interval of *historical time* into which they are born, grow up and old; and, second, within the company of their *coevals* (other individuals of the same, or similar, calendar age). As a consequence of their cohort's location in historical time, individuals and their coevals share an exposure to certain experiences and opportunities and are excluded from others.

Despite the notion of 'generation' (meaning cohort) being a popular folk model conceptualization of the differences in experiences, opportunities, and, often, 'world views' of people of various ages, contemporary sociologists have been rather inattentive towards it. Of course, cohort studies have been undertaken on a variety of topics, including fertility, education, employment, health and social mobility. The box below provides details of a well-known cohort study, the National Child Development Study. Since cohort studies follow samples over a period

---

THE NATIONAL CHILD DEVELOPMENT STUDY

The National Child Development Study (NCDS) takes as its subjects all persons living in Great Britain who were born between 3 and the 9 March 1958: a cohort of 17,000 children. A perinatal study was carried out in 1958 and subsequent studies were completed when the cohort were aged 7, 11, 16, 23, and 33. Up to age 16, data were collected from administrative records, from interviews with the mother and from postal surveys of teachers, doctors and others with direct knowledge of the cohort members. Information was obtained on the health, educational, social, and economic circumstances of the sample. At age 23, interviews were held with cohort members themselves, where they were asked about their educational and work histories since age 16, marital and family formation histories, their current circumstances, health, activities, and attitudes. These issues were also the focus of the fifth follow-up study, when the cohort members were aged 33.

Sources: Hakim 1987; Ferri 1993.

---

of time, they may offer explanations of the nature of social and political change and the effects of human ageing (Glenn 1977). Other studies, in following the experiences of young people in the transition from school to work, for example, document what are essentially 'cohort' problems: the common experiences of education, unemployment, and employment within particular historical periods (for example, Willis 1977; Wallace 1987). Nevertheless, the social significance of age as cohort has rarely been the focus of cohort studies (or, rather, studies which have cohorts as their sample). As was argued at the beginning of this chapter, such studies have tended to have other areas of primary concern (say, social mobility or the labour market) and it is to these other areas that empirical and theoretical contributions have primarily been made.

There are, though, several examples of theories which are primarily concerned with the social significance of age as cohort. In fact, there is a tradition of theorizing the nature and significance of cohorts that can be traced back to the ancient Greek philosophers (Nash 1978), and which includes the writings of Ortega y Gasset (Spitzer 1973) and the work of the French *Annales* school (Esler 1984). However, it is Karl Mannheim's (1952) essay 'The Problem of Generations' which is widely regarded as the most systematic and fully developed treatment of the cohort aspect of the ageing process from a sociological perspective (Bengtson, Furlong, and Laufer 1974). Mannheim's use of the term 'generation' is in the sense of 'cohort'. This would be the more accurate term to employ, but in the following discussion and subsequently, 'social' is placed before all instances of Mannheim's use of 'generation'. In this manner, account is taken of the need to be careful in use of terminology whilst links are maintained with sociological, and cultural, traditions which refer to 'generation', meaning cohort. A second reason for introducing the concept of social generation is that Mannheim's theory in fact represents an *elaboration* of the concept of cohort. Recognition that individuals belong to a cohort sensitizes us to the fact that their location in historical time exposes them to certain experiences, crises, and events and excludes them from others. Mannheim takes this idea further. He suggests that there is a key period of exposure, namely, during youth, which has lasting *ideological* effects. In other words, Mannheim's argument is that, as a result of differential exposure and exclusion due to location in historical time, there exist different social generations, each having distinctive world views. This, in turn, leads people of different ages to experience the *same* social and cultural events *differently*.

Like the life course approach, cohort and social generational perspectives have been praised for grasping the relationships between history and biography within society (Rosow 1978; Pilcher 1994a). However, a number of criticisms can be directed at Mannheim's theory, many of them arising from his attempt to take the concept of cohort one step further. One criticism relates to Mannheim's identification of youth as the key period during which social generations are formed. Clearly, this assumption is heavily reliant on the validity of the relationship between stages of the ageing process and key periods of socialization: people are 'fixed' within a socio-historical world that predominated in their youth and they carry this with them throughout their lives. Although the importance of youth as a period during which social and political outlooks are formed is supported by the findings of developmental psychology (Braungart 1984), the extent to which outlooks formed in youth subsequently remain unchanged throughout an individuals lifetime is less well-supported (Rosenmayr 1982). As Alwin and colleagues (1991) conclude, it remains a matter of debate whether the residues of early cohort experiences inscribe an indelible mark on the content of socio-political orientations in later life to the extent suggested by Mannheim (see discussion in Chapter Eight).

A more general criticism can be directed at both the cohort and social generational perspectives: the difficulty of distinguishing between three 'time effects': of individual ageing, of historical or period effects, and of cohort effects. Consider the following example involving the holding of driving licences. Few women in a cohort now aged 70–5 years old are likely to hold a driving licence. This may be an *age* effect; that is, as the women have grown older, they have given up their driving licences. It may be a *period* effect; due to (hypothetically) high levels of government investment in public transport, combined with punitive costs applied to the use of private cars, numbers holding driving licences may have fallen across *all* ages and cohorts. Finally, it may be a *cohort* effect: few women of their age ever learnt to drive in the first place because it simply was not expected of women in the past. In order to be in a position to specify precisely which effect explains the low level of driving licence holding amongst a cohort of women now aged 70, a study would have to have data on the level of licence holding amongst the cohort at earlier points in their lives. The study would also have to draw in at least one further cohort of women (also followed up until they were aged 70–5) who would be unaffected by the (hypothetical) period effect of high levels of investment in public transport; and who would also be unaffected by the cohort effect of gender norms discouraging women drivers. Clearly, the precise disentangling of the three time elements present in cohort and social generational studies would necessitate a complex, lengthy, and costly research design. This difficulty associated with the cohort and social generational perspectives underlines once again the complexity of age as a sociological phenomenon. To paraphrase Riley (1984), if people did grow up and grow old in laboratories, the investigation of ageing would be simplified. The fact that people grow up and grow old within society and within history means that much complexity surrounds the empirical investigation and theoretical explanation of the social significance of age. Despite the difficulties of researching cohort and social generational phenomena, studies of various stages of the life course have been influenced by these perspectives, including youth (Chapter Four). Evidence on the influence cohort and social generational processes have upon experiences and opportunities, culture and socio-political orientations, is reviewed in Chapter Eight, where Mannheim's theory is also considered in more detail.

Functionalist Perspectives

In keeping with their primary interest, functionalist theories on age are concerned with the *functions* age differentiation is seen to have for society as a whole. In the writings of Parsons (1954*a*) and Eisenstadt (1956), age differentiation is argued to be of great importance, both for the functioning of the social system and for the individual personality.

In the functionalist perspective, age and interage group relations are explained in terms of their relationships with *other* societal institutions and in terms of the role they play in contributing to social *continuity*. For the social system, age serves as a category for the distribution and allocation of roles. Age acts in these ways across the institutions that make up the social structure. It is therefore an important 'connecting link and organising point of reference' in relation to the other structural elements of the social system, including the kinship, educational, and occupational structures (Parsons 1954*a*). Age differentiation is seen to be important for social continuity, via the mechanism of parent–child socialization. The shift in age roles that is a necessary feature of moving from being a child to a parent also represents a shift from 'receiver' to 'transmitter' of cultural traditions. This shift in age roles is, therefore, essential to the ongoing continuity of the social system over time (Eisenstadt 1956). For the individual personality, awareness of one's age is argued to be an important integrative element, through its influence on an individual's self-identification. Eisenstadt (1956) argues that 'age awareness', or the awareness of age norms and age roles, serves as an important basis for both the individual's self-perception and for role expectations toward other individuals.

The functionalist perspective on age and interage group relations indicates how different age groups in society are structured in relation to one another. It points to the important role intergenerational relationships play, via socialization, in the transmission of cultural heritage (and hence social continuity) over time. The theory is useful in highlighting the fact that age is a basis on which roles and responsibilities are distributed in families, in the education system and the occupational structure. Functionalist theories on age also point to the importance of age for issues of identity, as a social category which is used to anticipate and understand the actions of other individuals, as well as a guide for their own behaviour by individuals themselves.

There are a number of criticisms that can be made against functionalist perspectives on age and generation, many of which can also be directed at functionalism in general. First, these theories are often teleological, explaining age differentiation in terms of its effects, clearly a somewhat circular argument. Secondly, it is deterministic, in that the actions and behaviour of individuals and groups tend to be explained in terms of the needs of a reified social system. Such an approach underemphasizes the active subjectivity of individuals and the *meanings* and interpretations placed by them upon age and interage group relations. Thirdly, functionalist perspectives neglect issues of power, inequality, and conflict between age groups. For example, Eisenstadt writes that relations between different age groups are 'necessarily asymmetrical' (1956: 30) from the point of view of authority and respect. He thus ignores the ways in which the apparent value consensus as to this state of affairs may reflect the interests of powerful and dominant groups within society, who find it advantageous to have age relations organized in such a way. Finally, although showing some sensitivity to cultural and historical contexts, functionalist perspectives suggest a universally valid theory of age and age relations, and so ultimately pay insufficient attention to culture and history. Despite these weaknesses, functionalist perspectives on age and age group relations have had considerable influence, particularly on the study of childhood, youth, and old age.

Political Economy Perspectives

Jones and Wallace (1992) criticize some examples of the life course perspective for losing sight of structural inequalities and the continuities of social reproduction. There is a grouping of Marxist influenced theoretical perspectives within the sociology of age which have issues of structural inequalities at the centre of their concerns. I refer to them here as 'political economy' perspectives, because their focus is on the 'interaction between the economic and political structure in society and the way they affect the distribution of resources and social goods' (Bond *et al.* 1990: 32). This theoretical approach to the social significance of age is most closely associated with the study of old age (see Chapter Six). It can, though, be argued to be implicit in much sociological theorizing and research on all stages of the life course and interage group relations, given its fundamental premiss that age is primarily socially, rather than biologically, constructed.

The political economy perspective on old age has been clearly set out by Estes (1986). The main aspects of this account can be applied more widely in order to characterize the approach of the perspective to the study of age and age relations as a whole. The main concern of political economy perspectives is to develop an understanding of the character and significance of variations in the treatment of age groups. It tries to relate these variations in treatment to the overall socio-economic, political, and cultural contexts in which people live. The perspective allows us to understand that, for example, the legal exclusion of children and persons over retirement age from the labour market in Britain is the outcome of social and political practices within a context of structural inequality. Young people and old people thus share a status of 'structured dependency' as a result of their restricted access to social resources, particularly income (Bond *et al.* 1990: 32). The important argument made by political economy perspectives is that inequalities in the distribution of resources should be understood in relation to the distribution of power within society, rather than in terms of individual variation (Arber and Ginn 1991).

Political economy perspectives have been criticized for concentrating their analyses of the treatment of age groups in terms of class relations within capitalist societies (Turner 1989) and for neglecting differences between capitalist societies in the treatment of age groups (Blakemore and Boneham 1994). More recently, though, attention has been paid to ways in which capitalist societies structure age in relation to gender (Arber and Ginn 1991) and to race and ethnicity (Blakemore and Boneham 1994). In this book, the 'structured dependency' of children, youth, and old people is considered in the relevant chapters, whilst class-based explanations of youth cultures are discussed in Chapter Four. Political economy perspectives have also influenced the study of mid-life, as is shown in Chapter Five.

Interpretive Perspectives

Although having a rather more diffuse and generalized influence than perspectives considered so far (Bond *et al.* 1990), interpretive perspectives have had an important impact on the ways in which age has been studied within sociology. Interpretive perspectives, including symbolic interactionism and phenomenology, propose that individuals act toward the world in terms of *meanings*. Meanings are derived from processes of definition and interpretation in social situations, which take place in or through interaction with other human beings.

Interpretivist perspectives are concerned, then, with *understanding* the meaning social phenomena have for individuals and with the *processes* through which individuals interpret and understand the social world. For Prout and James (1990), interpretive sociology has influenced the sociological study of age (particularly childhood) in two main ways. First, it has encouraged a critical reflection on, and hence, sociological analysis of, aspects of social reality which were previously taken for granted and considered as 'natural'. Second, it has encouraged an understanding that social life is an accomplishment of human beings and carried out on the basis of beliefs, perspectives, and typifications. 'These two features of interpretive sociology have combined to create a particular interest in the perspectives of low status groups', including children and older people (Prout and James 1990: 15). Generally, then, interpretivist perspectives within the sociology of age are concerned with the *meanings* individuals attach to age, both in terms of their own subjective age-identities and in their interactions with others. Interpretivist perspectives have influenced the study of, for example, subjective age-identities amongst older people and stereotypes and images of old age (Chapter Six).

Like the life course perspective, interpretive approaches can be criticized for neglecting structural inequalities and the continuities of social reproduction. However, it can also be argued that theories which do focus on these issues themselves neglect phenomena which interpretivist approaches are concerned with. In the end, then, different theoretical positions offer different explanations of the social significance of age and each makes an important contribution to a fuller sociological understanding of age and interage group relationships.

This chapter has reviewed five theoretical perspectives which are concerned with one, or more, of the main aspects of the ageing process (as outlined in Chapter One), and/or which have influenced the way in which sociological studies of age and interage group relations have been conducted. Other theories have been applied to particular stages of the life course or to the nature of age relationships, including exchange theory (Turner 1989) and Weber's theory of patriarchy (Hood-Williams 1990). Exchange theory is discussed in the chapter on 'Later Life and Old Age' (Chapter Six). Hood-Williams's application of the concept of patriarchy to analyse power relations in children's lives is considered in Chapter Three.

Whilst the five main theoretical perspectives reviewed in this chapter are each distinctive in their conceptions of the social world and in the contributions they make to the understanding of age, they can be divided into two on the basis of their shared fundamental emphases. Functionalist, political economy, and cohort/social generational perspectives all share a *structuralist* emphasis, in that they argue that the social significance of age, in various ways, is the result of the organization and structure of society. In the case of functionalist approaches, the social significance of age arises out of the needs of an interconnected, consensually organized social system. From a political economy perspective, variations in the treatment of age groups are a consequence of structural inequalities of power and resources. Cohort and social generational perspectives emphasize the importance of *historical* social structures in shaping the social significance of age over time. The fundamental emphasis shared by the life course and interpretive perspectives is a concern with individuals, with the processual nature of social reality and the role of meanings in its construction. In assessing theoretical perspectives on age, cohort, and generation, it is important to remember that 'no one theory is a completely accurate representation of reality' but that 'some provide better insight into a particular phenomenon than others' (Bond *et al.* 1990: 18).

It is clear that the development of sociological theorizing on age and interage group relationships cannot be understood outside wider developments, both within sociology as a discipline and in society as a whole. The dominant paradigm of functionalism in the 1950s exerted and continues to exert, a strong influence on social theories of age. As critiques of functionalism grew from the 1960s onwards, so alternative perspectives on age and interage group relations emerged, drawing on Marxist and interpretivist sociologies. Over time, there has been a gradual trend toward *contextualizing* ageing processes, within culture, the economy, politics, and history. Theorizing on age has also been influenced by developments in wider society, including economic booms and recessions, demographic changes and altered political climates. For example, the various liberation movements of the 1960s and 1970s included a concern with the oppression of people based on their age and this can be seen to have contributed to a questioning of the 'naturalness' of age divisions and an awareness of the possibility of changing the ways in which age relations are organized. It would seem, then, that like age itself, theories about age are best understood in the socio-historical contexts of their production.

Further Reading

For an account of the main theoretical positions within sociology, see Lee and Newby (1983). The volumes edited by Allatt *et al.* (1987) and Bryman *et al.* (1987) show how widely the life course perspective can be used in sociology. Glenn (1977) is an informative account of cohort analysis, whilst Abrams (1982) has a highly readable section on social generation.

Chapter Three

Children and Childhood

If the life course is a way of conceptualizing the process of growing up and growing old, then 'childhood' is a way of conceptualizing the 'growing up' stage of that process. To characterize childhood in this way, though, is thoroughly value-laden. As Hockey and James (1993) point out, 'growing up' operates as an orientational metaphor, one which encapsulates the way in which childhood is commonly perceived as a preparation for the *central* stage of the life course; that is, for adulthood. Children are 'growing up' toward adulthood. Thinking about children primarily in terms of what they will eventually become is widespread. It is clearly apparent in the ways in which children have been studied, both by sociologists and other academics. Of all the stages in the life course discussed in this book, childhood has probably been the most extensively studied. However, it has been studied in particular ways, with the issue of the development of children being the overriding concern. Generally, studies have been undertaken very much with a view to what children will eventually become, rather than in and of themselves.

It is far from being the case, then, that children are absent from sociological theory and research. Rather, they are present in particular ways and rarely in their own right. We might say that children and childhood have been viewed in an 'adult-centric' way. In sociology, the dominance of functionalist perspectives has meant that children have mostly been studied in terms of their *socialization* into adults. Two early texts on the sociology of childhood are almost entirely concerned with childhood as a stage of socialization and children as receptacles of adult teaching (Ritchie and Koller 1964; Shipman 1972). Children as active, reactive, and interactive individuals with an important role to play in shaping the social world (rather than simply being shaped by adults) have been overlooked by the sociological gaze. Until recently, it has been difficult to find children's voices and perspectives, even within sociological literature on family and domestic life, and education and the school. As Chisholm and her colleagues (1990: 5) describe it, the sociology of childhood 'remains in its own infancy'.

This chapter aims to complete one of the most basic, but none the less important, tasks of a sociology of childhood, which is to make commonsense thinking about what children are, and how they should be treated, appear 'strange'. It does this in three main ways. First, historical evidence is examined which suggests that ideas about children and how they should be treated have not always been as they are now. Second, the socially constructed nature of childhood is further emphasized through a consideration of cross-cultural evidence. In these ways, childhood is shown to be specific to historical and cultural contexts, rather than a universal and natural state. Third, relationships between adults and children in modern Britain are examined in terms of issues of power, control, and dependency. As Hood-Williams (1990) argues, this approach opens up a hidden aspect of family life and provides an important stimulus for problematizing the concept of childhood. Issues of power, control, and dependency in adult–child relations inevitably lead to a discussion of the notion of children's 'rights'. The chapter draws to a close with an assessment of trends toward an increase in children's rights and the argument that, as a consequence, childhood in modern Britain is 'disappearing'.

Childhood in Modern Britain

Before historical and cross-cultural comparisons can be drawn, it is first necessary to give a brief account of the form childhood takes in modern British society. In contemporary British society, childhood appears to be a clear and distinct stage of life. It is largely taken for granted that the lives of 'children' (chronologically defined as those under 16 years of age) should be organized in a radically different manner from the lives of 'adults'. The status differences between children and adults are emphasized and regulated in a number of ways. To begin with, the lives of children are *legally regulated* according to their specific chronological ages within childhood. For example, at the age of 5, children must go to school or receive some other form of full-time education. Moreover, children must remain in school or continue to receive full-time education until they are 16. At the age of 5, children can legally drink alcohol in private but they cannot drink alcohol in public houses until they are 18 (although they may drink alcohol if they are also having a meal once they are 16). At the age of 14 children must pay the full (i.e. adult) fare on public transport. At age 13, children can get a part-time job, as long as it lasts not more than two hours per day. There are numerous other examples of the ways in which the lives of children, what they are required to do, and what they are permitted to do, are legally regulated according to their chronological age within childhood.

There are other ways, too, in which children are marked out as having a separate status from adults. For example, the ways in which children are dressed differs from the ways in which adults dress. Clothes are designed and styled specifically for children and there are clothes shops devoted exclusively to 'children's wear'. It is not merely a question of scale, of children's clothes being smaller versions of adults' clothes. Particularly for infants and younger children, children's clothes are distinctive from those styled for adults: in colours, in fabrics, in design, in 'cuteness'. Aside from clothes, there are a myriad other industries which specialize in the manufacture of products or the provision of services to children. There is the children's toy industry and toy shops. There are specialist publishers of children's books and children's comics. There is a whole snack food and fast food industry which markets its products directly at children. Furniture, wallpaper, and duvet covers are designed specifically for children. There are television programmes, television channels, and movies, all directing their output to children as an audience. Public areas of open space are fenced off as children's 'play areas' and specialized equipment is provided for their amusement and enjoyment. Adult public spaces, such as public houses and, increasingly, supermarkets may also have designated 'children's areas'. In these various ways, children are marked out as persons of a special status, with special needs and requirements separate to those of adults.

Ennew (1986) has argued that the modern form of childhood has two main aspects. First, it is characterized by a rigid age hierarchy which permeates the whole of society and so creates a distance between adults and children. The status difference between adults and children is expressed and enhanced in various ways, as illustrated above. Ennew suggests that this separation of adults from children can be understood as a 'quarantine period', a period which keeps children in a space away from the 'nasty infections' of adulthood, including sex, violence, and commerce. This leads to the second aspect of modern childhood identified by Ennew: that it is seen as a 'golden age', a stage of life that should be characterized by happiness and innocence. Childhood in British society is celebrated as the one good, free, happy stage of life. Children are, though, vulnerable and in need of protection from the malevolent adult world. In addition to the various ways in which the status differences between children and adults are legally regulated, enhanced, and emphasized, the lives of children are lived out in family contexts, where adults as parents materially provide for children and protect them from the threatening adult world. Second, children's lives are lived out in school or educational settings, where their role is that of pupil with adults as teachers. Third, children's lives are lived through leisure and play, rather than through participation in formal paid employment. The role of worker is an adult one from which children need protecting. The three arenas in which modern childhood takes place can be seen as spaces which, although populated by adults, serve both to protect children from, and prepare them for, adulthood.

The notion of 'separateness' emerges as the most important feature of modern conceptions of childhood (Ennew 1986; Archard 1993). It encapsulates the variety of ways in which distinctions are drawn and then emphasized between persons who are 'children' and persons who are 'adults'. Underlying the notion of separateness is the assumption that children have a unique nature which distinguishes them from adults. In particular, childhood is regarded as a stage of incompetence, a stage characterized by a lack of the capacity, skills, and power of adulthood (Archard 1993). In many ways, then, childhood is defined in opposition to adulthood (Alanen 1988).

Childhood in modern Britain is a status which is protected from the adult world by adults themselves. When subjected to sociological scrutiny, childhood begins to be revealed as a largely social invention and not just a natural state. There is, in fact, very little about the nature of children that is natural and universal. Of course, there are observable physiological criteria which distinguish children from adults: in their physical capacities, linguistic abilities, reasoning abilities, and sexual development. Ennew (1986) marks out three 'pre-adult stages' on the basis of differential capacities and abilities but argues that differences between 'infant' and 'adult' are the most extensive. Those stages in between are blurred and vary according to culture. To take a sociological perspective on childhood is not to deny that children are physiologically immature compared to adults. On the contrary, to take a sociological perspective on childhood is to recognize that the way in which that immaturity is understood and made meaningful varies over time and place and is a fact of culture (Prout and James 1990). Biological or physiological immaturity is a universal and largely inescapable natural phenomenon but it is the interpretations placed upon children's bodies that sociologists are primarily interested in. In Western cultures, as Hockey and James (1993) explain, children are defined primarily by their bodies, which are interpreted as signifiers of their perceived vulnerability and dependency. The child's body is seen as deficient and as lacking the skills and abilities of the adult body. Moreover, the positive skills and qualities that children do possess as physiologically immature beings, such as health, vitality, energy and enthusiasm, are sentimentalized and seen as something they will 'grow out' of—and thus as a further sign of their immaturity. Hockey and James's (1993) argument is that children's bodies are 'read' in a selective and culturally specific way in Western societies, a 'reading' which forms the basis for the Western conceptualization of childhood as 'separate' and children as vulnerable and dependent. Other cultural traditions 'read' children's bodies differently and define adult–child relations differently, and so differences between children as a class of persons and adults as a class of persons are less marked.

Childhood has to be understood as a social construction, as a way of understanding and making sense of the early period of the human life span which varies across cultures and across time. Contemporary Western notions of children as 'separate', as innocent, happy, apolitical, asexual, vulnerable, as in need of protection and dependent, and of childhood as lived out in family settings, educational settings, and through leisure and play—all of these notions about what children are and what childhood is need to be recognized as culturally and historically specific. As the following sections illustrate, all societies at all historical times have made some distinction between 'childhood' and 'adulthood'. But where the lines are drawn, and how the lines are drawn, varies considerably, as does the degree of emphasis made between the one and the other.

Childhood in History

Aries's (1962) *Centuries of Childhood* is the standard reference point for any discussion of the history of childhood. In his book, Aries is concerned to address the question of how 'ignorance of childhood' in the tenth century gradually changed into the 'preoccupation' and 'obsession' with childhood in modern societies. Aries summarizes his own thesis as follows.

In medieval society the idea of childhood did not exist; this is not to suggest that children were neglected, forsaken, or despised. The idea of childhood is not to be confused with affection for children: it corresponds to an awareness of the particular nature of childhood, that particular nature which distinguishes the child from the adult, even the young adult. In medieval society, this awareness was lacking. That is why, as soon as the child could live without the constant solicitude of his mother . . . he belonged to adult society. (Aries 1962: 125)

As his evidence, Aries uses depictions of children in paintings and other forms of medieval art as well as documentary evidence, particularly a diary of the childhood of Louis XIII. In medieval paintings, Aries argues, children appear without 'any of the characteristics of childhood: they have simply been depicted on a smaller scale' (1962: 31). The ways in which children dressed, for example, did not distinguish them from adults. The paintings also suggest that children mingled with adults in everyday life and that any gathering for the purpose of work, relaxation, or sport brought together both children and adults (1962: 36). This integration of children into the adult world extended to sexual matters. Aries quotes from a diary of the childhood of Louis XIII to illustrate that sex was not regarded as a matter to be hidden from children. The touching of children's genitals, both by themselves and adults, was commonplace, as were discussions of sexual organs, matters of pregnancy, and sexual reproduction.

Aries is not suggesting that the physiological immaturity of the early stage of the human life span went completely unrecognized in medieval society. Clearly, a dependent stage of infancy existed and these children were recognized as fragile, vulnerable, and in need of their mother's (or other carer's) 'constant solicitude'. Indeed, Aries suggests that the fragility and vulnerability of children, resulting in high rates of infant mortality, was one reason why medieval society was 'ignorant of childhood'. The chance of children dying meant that 'people could not allow themselves to become too attached to something that was regarded as a probable loss' (Aries 1962: 37). What Aries is suggesting is that, once children had passed the age of 5 or so, their bodies no longer signified their fragility and vulnerability to the same extent. Subsequently, children were regarded as adults, albeit smaller in size, and became integrated into the adult world. 'Childhood' in medieval times was of a brief duration, ending at a time when contemporary childhood is marked by transition into primary school.

According to Aries, the discovery of childhood in the modern sense first began in the thirteenth century and evolved gradually until the end of the sixteenth century, when evidence of its development becomes more plentiful and significant. In the seventeenth century, the child ceased to be dressed like an adult and had 'an outfit reserved for his own age group, which set him apart from adults' (1962: 48). Aries's use of the masculine pronoun is significant here because the attempt to distinguish children from adults by means of their clothing was first confined to boys; boys were the first 'specialized children' (1962: 56). This change in children's dress was also differentiated by class, occurring first in middle class or aristocratic families. Children of the lower classes 'kept up the old way of life which made no distinction between children and adults, in dress or in work or in play' (1962: 59).

Aries's argument, then, is that from the sixteenth and seventeenth centuries onwards significant changes took place in general attitudes toward children and a key factor in this was the growing influence of Christianity. Churchmen and moralists elaborated the new concept of childhood, which saw children, due to their sweetness and simplicity, become a source of amusement and relaxation for adults, adding a concern with children as fragile 'creatures of God' who needed discipline, reforming, and safeguarding. Thus began the removal of the child from adult society, a process reinforced through changes resulting in the separation of the consumption and production functions of the family, the privatization of family life, and the growth of formalized, institutionally based education in the eighteenth and nineteenth centuries.

Various criticisms have been made of Aries's thesis, including a questioning of the sources he used as regards their validity and representativeness. The most important criticisms, though, relate to Aries's value-ladeness (Archard 1993). Aries states quite emphatically that in medieval societies the idea of childhood did not exist. As one critic puts it, Aries claims to disclose an *absence* of the idea of childhood, whereas he should only claim to find a *dissimilarity* in ideas about childhood between past and present (Archard 1993). Certainly, Aries can claim to have shown that medieval societies lacked twentieth-century notions of childhood. This is not to say that such societies therefore lacked any concept of childhood whatsoever. In criticism of Aries, Pollock writes that 'even if children were regarded differently in the past, this does not mean they were not regarded as children' (1983: 263). Another related criticism of Aries is that he takes modern conceptions of childhood for granted, implying that the ways in which children are treated and their lives organized in modern societies is 'good' and 'proper' (Archard 1993). This assumption is not shared by writers who regard the 'separateness' of modern childhood as an enforced and unnatural 'segregation' (e.g. Firestone 1979).

Although there is some debate on the validity of Aries's thesis, there is widespread agreement that modern conceptions of childhood differ from those held in the past, and that the particular forms that childhood takes varies according to historical context. Hendrick, for example, traces nine constructions and reconstructions of childhood in

Britain from 1800 to the present day. His aim is to illustrate the historical variability of the concept of childhood and to show that perceptions
of childhood produced over the last few centuries can only be understood in the context of how different cohorts responded to the social,
economic, religious, and political challenges of their respective eras
(Hendrick 1990: 36). Hendrick's conclusion is that the different constructions of childhood have the shared intention to express, from the
adult perspective, a desirable state of childhood, what its essential and
natural qualities are, and how best to protect and control it (1990: 55).

One way of charting the emergence of modern conceptions of childhood is by looking at changes in legislation. The various Factory Acts of
the nineteenth century progressively restricted and excluded children
from particular forms or hours of work (although it is important to
remember, as Hendrick (1990) points out, that objections were directed
at certain forms of employment for certain age groups of children,
rather than at child labour as a whole). More or less in parallel with their
progressive exclusion from employment, the various Education Acts of
the nineteenth century gradually enclosed children within the world of
school. In 1880, education was made compulsory for children under
the age of 10. In 1902, education was made compulsory for all children
aged between 5 and 12 years old. In the twentieth century, the mini-
mum school leaving age has gradually increased, from 14 in 1918, to 15
in 1947, and to 16 in 1972. It was not until the mid-eighteenth century
that legislation began to distinguish between criminal offences committed by children and those committed by adults. Up until this point,
children were held to be morally and criminally responsible for their
own actions and were consequently punished in the same ways as
adults, including via the death penalty, transportation, and imprison-
ment.

Historical analyses reveal that modern understandings of children as
having specialized needs and requirements and as 'separate' from
adults are relatively recent developments. Even the commonly used
chronological marker of childhood ending at age 16 only dates back to
1972. Whilst the physiological immaturity of children's bodies was not
marked in medieval paintings other than by their relative smallness, in
eighteenth-century Britain, the physiological immaturity was interpreted as making lower-class children well suited to particular forms of
labour, including as chimney sweeps. In modern Britain, the very same
physiological immaturity of children's bodies continues to have significance. It is now interpreted, though, as a signifier of the vulnerability
of children and an indication of their need for nurturing care and protection; consequently, the idea of child labour is morally repugnant.

The modern conception of childhood as 'institutionalized separateness' has emerged gradually over several centuries in Britain. It has not enveloped all categories of children (female, male, the lower classes, rural and urban children) in exactly the same ways and at exactly the same points in history. Nevertheless, the direction of change has been toward an increasing division in British society between the world of the child and the world of the adult, and a lengthening of the chronological markers assigned to childhood.

Childhood: a Cross-Cultural Perspective

Much of the historical debate about childhood has focused on its emergence in European societies. Aside from looking at how ideas about childhood have changed over time in one cultural tradition, another means of critically analysing childhood in modern Britain is to draw upon evidence from other cultures.

A useful point of reference for cross-cultural perspectives on childhood is Ruth Benedict's (1955) paper, first published in 1938. Benedict emphasizes at the outset of her discussion that, although ageing is a fact of nature, the way in which the transition from childhood to adulthood is accomplished varies from one society to another. Her argument is focused on childhood and adult–child relationships. She groups together evidence under three headings: the responsible–non-responsible role, dominance–submission, and sexual roles. Benedict cites her own evidence to draw contrasts with the Western experience. Here, I illustrate Benedict's points with evidence from other studies.

The responsible–non-responsible role

Here, Benedict considers evidence from cultures where children are expected to have responsible roles from an early age. They learn responsible social participation through engaging in tasks which they are capable of. Holmes (1974), in his study of a Samoan village, found that being 'too young' was never given as a reason for not allowing a child to undertake a given task. 'Whether it be the handling of dangerous tools, the carrying of extremely heavy loads of produce . . . if a child thinks he can handle the activity, parents do not object' (1974: 79).

Dominance–submission

Benedict argues that the expectation of children's responsible status role is accompanied by low priority placed upon their obedience and submission to the will of adults. Firth's (1970) study of the Tikopia, an island people of the remote Western Pacific, found that little action was taken to compel the obedience of children. Their individuality was respected and considerable freedom allowed. 'Conforming to the will of a senior is regarded as a concession to be granted, not a right to be expected; an adult behaves to a child as one free spirit to another' (1970: 88).

Sexual roles

Here, Benedict refers to cultures which view children's sexual play as innocuous, and as of no serious consequence. One study of Australian aborigines in the 1920s reported that sexual games formed an important part of children's conversation and play, including acting out sexual intercourse and engaging in masturbation. Such behaviour was not, apparently, censured by adults and seemed not to be a matter of concern to them (Roheim 1974).

Benedict's central argument is that, in some cultures, there is much less of a marked discontinuity between behaviours expected within the childhood and adult stages of the life course than is the case in Western societies. Evidence from other cultures serves to emphasize that 'childhood' varies over geographical space and cultural traditions, as well as over historical time.

Power, Control, and Dependency in Modern British Childhood

Cross-cultural evidence indicates that, in some societies around the world, children are minimally subjected to adult control and have important and responsible roles to play within their communities, including economically. In such societies, adult–child relations are organized in ways which may appear 'strange' from the modern Western perspective. This section returns to a focus on modern British childhood. By examining adult–child relations in terms of the distribution of power, control, and resources, it aims to make modern British childhood itself appear 'strange'.

Earlier in this Chapter it was argued that modern childhood takes the form of an institutionalized separation of the world of children from the world of adults. In Ennew's (1986) words, there is a 'rigid age hierarchy' which permeates the whole of society, creating a distance between adults and children. 'Separateness', then, can be emphasized as the most important feature of modern conceptions of childhood. This 'separateness', expressed through a whole range of cultural practices which accentuate it, is grounded in the assumption that children have an especial and particular nature which clearly and distinctly sets them apart from adults. Childhood is characterized as a stage of incompetence and incompleteness, in comparison to adulthood. Children are seen to lack the capacities, skills, and competencies of adults. As a consequence of this immaturity in terms of skills and competency, children are seen to require their own distinct and separate world in which they can grow up and eventually achieve adulthood along with the power, skills, and competencies that define it. It is because children are defined in terms of their lack of competency and relative immaturity, compared to adults, that they are viewed as legitimately vulnerable, legitimately dependent, and legitimately in need of protection, surveillance, and control by adults. It is the understanding of childhood as incompleteness and separateness from adulthood which underpins, or provides the basis for, the differential distribution of power, responsibility, and resources between children and adults in modern society.

The emergence of modern conceptions of childhood has been marked by an increasing institutionalization of asymmetrical relations of power between children and adults. With the development of the privatized nuclear family, children have become increasingly subject to parental authority and control, whilst the expansion of compulsory schooling has seen children become subject to the authority and control by teachers, who act *in loco parentis*. Relations of dependency between children and adults and the differential distribution of resources have also become progressively more marked through the exclusion of children from formal paid employment (Hockey and James 1993). Participation in the labour force is an important component of the Western conception of independent 'personhood'. Those groups, including children and the elderly, who do not participate in the labour market and are, therefore, dependent, are seen to have a lesser claim to personhood (Hockey and James 1993).

Economic Dependency

In modern Britain, children are kept economically unproductive in that their access to paid employment is controlled and restricted (see box opposite). Of course, children do engage in certain types of work, although this work is often disregarded and not perceived as 'real' or 'proper' work (Hockey and James 1993). For example, children may work informally in their homes undertaking domestic work. Outside domestic environments, children are likely to work in low-paid, marginal jobs such as baby-sitting or newspaper delivery. One study of 500 schoolgirls, most of whom were between the ages of 12 and 16, found that around one-third held a part-time job. Most worked in shops or did newspaper rounds or baby-sitting (Pilcher *et al.* 1989). Another study, which looked at boys and girls, found a similar proportion holding part-time jobs. Boys, however, were less likely to work in shops or to baby-sit but were more likely to deliver newspapers and undertake manual work (Balding 1987). Older children are more likely to engage in paid work than younger children. Nevertheless, the importance of the 'child labour market' is seldom recognized (Griffin 1985). The ideology of childhood places children outside the labour force and so their significant contribution to the wider economy is hidden (Hockey and James 1993). The kinds of work undertaken by children, as by other low-status groups such as the elderly and the disabled, reflects their position of 'structural marginality' (Hockey and James 1993). In other cultures, children are not as separated or marginalized from economically productive activity. They take on economically important work from what would be seen as an 'early age' in modern Britain. Evidence from the Sudan, for example, shows that children from the age of 3 or 4 delivered messages and carried food or other small items from house to house within their settlement. As children grew older, they assumed more and more responsibility, collecting wood or herding animals (Katz 1993). The Sudan study also shows that children participate in work *alongside* adults, carrying out activities appropriate to their abilities.

Children in modern Britain are denied access to substantial income from paid work and are denied control over financial resources. The marginal forms of work they are able to participate in bring minimal economic rewards. Parents may, or course, give 'pocket-money' to their children but often this money is 'tied' to expenditure only on certain items. Hockey and James (1993) point out that whilst theoretically children are in receipt of state benefit, in the form of child benefit paid to their mothers, children themselves have no direct access to this

---

CHILDREN AND YOUNG PERSONS ACT 1933

The Children and Young Persons Act 1933 limits the employment of children to those aged over 13 and under 16, and provides that no child may be employed before 7 a.m. or after 7 p.m. on any day, before the close of school, or for more than two hours on any day on which he/she is required to attend school; or more than two hours on any Sunday, or to lift, carry, or move anything so heavy as to be likely to cause injury.

Source: Fyfe 1989.

---

money. In contrast to British children's limited access to financial resources, Schildkrout (1978) found that children of the Hausa people in Nigeria become highly involved in the cash economy, engaging in running errands for money, street trading, and a variety of household tasks.

Power and Control in Adult–Child Relations

Hood-Williams (1990) has argued that examining adult–child relations in terms of issues of power, control, and dependency opens up hidden aspects of family life and provides an important stimulus to problematizing the concept of childhood. What hidden aspects of family life are revealed? In what ways do parent–child relations constitute power relations? The work of Hockey and James (1993) provides a general description of the ways in which adult–child relations can be understood as power relations. They argue that children are subject to regimes of control which effectively deny them much active choice or say in the direction of their own lives. Children are made dependent through strategies employed by adults in their roles as carers. Specifically, the care which parents have for their children is registered and expressed in their explicit control of children's behaviour and actions. Through such social practices, Hockey and James argue, full personhood is denied to children. They write that 'if personhood in Western society is symbolized through ideas of autonomy, self-determination and choice, these were the very options being edited out by those caring for the very young . . .' (1993: 3).

Hood-Williams (1990) draws upon Weber's theory of authority to analyse power relations in children's lives. He introduces the concept of 'age patriarchy', which refers to the authority relations between parents and children that are characterized by an imbalance of power, control, and resources. In addition to illustrating the ways in which children's work is marginalized and their access to financial resources is limited, Hood-Williams shows the importance of the 'principle of obedience' in adult–child relations. He cites the Newsons' (1976) study of parents of 7-year-old children, which seems to show the 'taken-for-granted' quality of the obedience principle: 'to be a child seems commonly to be an "immediate relationship" of command and obedience' (Hood-Williams 1990: 163). Despite the emergence of child-centred philosophies of parenting and education, Hood-Williams argues that within the home and the school, conventional power relations and the dependence of children remains. Children continue to be subject to the authority of adults, particularly their parents and their teachers. Children are expected to be obedient and to show respect to their elders. If obedience and respect are lacking, then children may be physically punished by their parents. Punishment may take other forms, such as the withdrawal of privileges—watching television or playing on the computer. The child may be 'grounded' and not be allowed out with friends or may be confined to a specified and restricted space, like a bedroom.

Space, time, and body: controls in age patriarchy

Adult control over children's *space* is one of three types of control which Hood-Williams argues is distinctive to age patriarchy. Controls over children's *bodies* and controls over children's *time* will be discussed shortly.

'Children's lives are highly localized and spatially restricted' (Hood-Williams 1990: 165). They are told to play in certain areas, within either the confines of the house or some other restricted geographical area. They are also told not to play or be present in other areas. Shops commonly display signs which say 'no unaccompanied children' or 'no schoolchildren', whilst public houses and such like also bar their presence. Many of the controls over children's space are, of course, practised by adults as *carers* to protect children from other adults. Katz (1993) compares the relative vastness of children's spatial range in rural Sudan with the limits placed on children in Western urban areas. The Sudanese children roamed widely and freely both within the village and to fields and wooded areas at its outskirts 5 kilometres away. In contrast, in urban spaces in industrialized settings, parental concerns over children's safety lead to severe spatial restrictions. Such children are heavily supervised in public spaces and so have their autonomy restricted. Data show significant increases in the numbers of British children whose parents drive them to and from school. Since 1971 the proportion of primary school children being chauffeured to school has gone up from one in ten to one in three (Hillman, Adams, and Whitelegg 1991), and this can be seen as a restriction on children's independent spatial mobility. As Figure 3.1 shows, children are less likely to go to school unaccompanied in 1990 than they were in 1971.

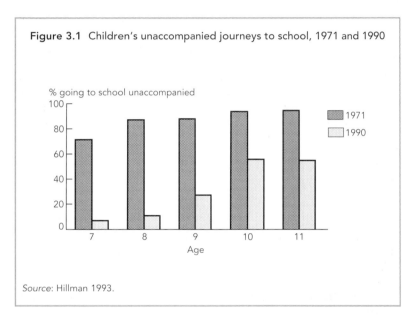

Figure 3.1 Children's unaccompanied journeys to school, 1971 and 1990

Source: Hillman 1993.

Recent concerns over children as delinquents and criminals have led to tighter surveillance over their presence in public spaces, especially at times when they should be in school spaces. In 1994, the Secretary of State for Education announced funding of £14 million for schemes to combat truancy. He praised Staffordshire County Council's 'Truancy Watch' scheme, which involved shopkeepers being asked to challenge and report young people they suspected of missing school (Macleod 1994).

Power relations in children's lives are also evident in the ways in which adults operate control over *time*. The daily temporal rhythm of children's lives is tightly controlled by adults. The amount of time spent on certain activities such as school work, watching television, or playing computer games is one area of control. Time spent in certain places is also regulated, so that there is a time to be at school and a time to come home. The times at which children should sleep, get up, and eat are all set by adults. Hood-Williams also points to the ways in which children's progression through childhood or their speed of growing up is controlled by adults. It is adults who define whether children are 'too young' or 'too old' to engage in certain activities or behave in certain ways. The age-graded education system can be seen as a means of controlling children's 'growing-up' time, and the recent national testing of children at 7, 11, and 14 as assessments of the 'speed' of their educational development. Children who progress through childhood 'too fast' are deemed to be 'precocious' and 'cheeky'.

The third area of distinctive control in children's lives identified by Hood-Williams is control over children's *bodies*. Indeed, Hood-Williams writes that 'Childhood seems remarkable for the degree of intervention onto the body of the child' (1990: 165). The way children sit, stand, walk, and run and *where* their bodies *are*, are all subject to adult authority. The clothes children wear, their hairstyles, whether they have their ears pierced, wear glasses, or sun hats, are also controlled by adults. The child's body is washed, cleaned, and fed by adults. It is routine and taken for granted that children's bodies can be touched (albeit in certain ways and by certain persons and not others). Children's heads can be patted, their hands held, they can be cuddled, kissed, and pulled onto laps or be picked up and held. Children's bodies may also be disciplined by adults, through 'smacking' or 'slapping'. A child's touching of its own body may also be regulated by adults, so that it is told not to play with its genitals, suck its thumb, or pick its nose.

As Hood-Williams (1990) notes, controls over children's time, space, and bodies are obviously interrelated: where a child is at a particular time and what she or he is wearing, for example, involves all three aspects of control. It is also clear that there are likely differences in space, time, and body control between children of different social classes, gender, ethnicity, and by urban-rural location. Figure 3.2 shows that there are marked differences by gender in children's independent spatial mobility. Other evidence suggests that the ethnic origin and gender of children are important in differentiating parental strictness with regard to time, space, and body controls. In a study of young people aged 15–16, parents of Asian origin were found to be more strict, particularly toward their daughters, than other groups of parents (Brannen *et al.* 1994). In general, though, evidence on this area is lacking. Nevertheless, whatever variations there are between different types of children, Hood-Williams argues that all children are subject to the principle of obedience to adults. The three aspects of control identified by Hood-Williams represent common sources of friction in adult–child relations, something which is revealing of the powerful controlling functions they have (Hockey and James 1993). Bedtime, clothing, and where children should and should not have been for example, are all issues that adults and children struggle over, with adults trying to assert their authority and command obedience, and children trying to resist.

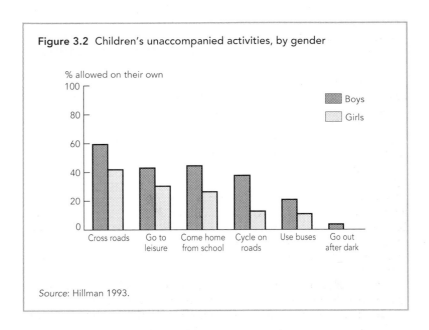

Figure 3.2 Children's unaccompanied activities, by gender

% allowed on their own

Source: Hillman 1993.

Examining adult–child relations in terms of power, control, and dependency allows an appreciation of the ways in which children struggle against the category of childhood. The resistance strategies employed by children against the confining and restrictive category of childhood are discussed by Hockey and James (1993). One such strategy is what Hockey and James term 'acting up', that is, acting as if they were adults by doing things that children aren't *meant* to do. For example, children may use swear words and sexual words, they may smoke cigarettes, drink alcohol, engage in sexual activity, or go so-called 'joy riding'. Hockey and James also point to the ways in which children continually anticipate the numerical growth that will make them eligible for the more powerful social category of 'adult'. Often, children exaggerate their calendar age ('I'm nearly 8'), or tell it with extreme preciseness ('I am 6 years and 7 months old').

Children may also resist adult's control through 'acting down', that is *retreating* from adult status. Hockey and James use the example of the way in which children may 'infantilize' themselves linguistically by reverting to 'baby talk', as in 'me want', or 'me can't' (1993: 164). Children may also refuse to walk, or demand to go to the toilet at inconvenient times, in order to resist adult control. On the basis of these sorts of strategies of resistance employed by children, Hockey and James conclude that childhood is a category from which most children want to escape. Children, in this view, are constantly struggling against the adult definition of childhood.

Examining adult–child relations in terms of issues of power, control, and dependency further reveals the historical and cultural specificity of modern childhood. In other cultures and at other times, children's *differing* abilities are stressed, rather than their lack of abilities compared to adults. Divisions between adults and children at other times and at other places are not so tightly drawn, defined, or controlled. Correspondingly, in other cultures and at other times, children do participate in economic life, they do have some control over financial resources, and they are not subject to the authority and control of adults to the same extent as most modern British children. As Jackson writes, 'Our children are asexual, apolitical, vulnerable, dependent, incapable of taking part in serious adult pursuits not because that is the way children naturally *are* but because that is they way they are treated' (1982: 28). Revealing the social construction of childhood raises the possibility of changing the way relations between adults and children are organized and the way children as an age group are treated in modern society. This issue is the focus of the rest of the Chapter.

Philosophies of Childhood

One of the strengths of sociology as a discipline is that in showing that social relations are not natural, fixed, and unchangeable, it opens up the possibility of change. Taking a sociological approach to the study of childhood raises the issue of alternative ways of organizing adult–child relations in modern society. The idea that there are other ways to be a child, other meanings to childhood as a stage in the life course, is evident in perspectives which stress that 'children are people too' and that they, as a consequence, should have the same rights and privileges as adults. The contention that children are people who should have the same rights as people (i.e. adults) is associated with the perspective that can be summarized as 'child liberationism'. In contrast, the 'liberal caretaking' perspective argues against the liberation of children via the extension of their rights. These two oppositional philosophies will now be discussed and here I draw heavily on Archard's (1993) account of them.

Representatives of child liberationism include Holt (1974) and Firestone (1979). Those who favour the modern conception of childhood regard the nuclear family and schooling as confirmation of children's special nature. Child liberationists, in contrast, see these developments as oppressive to children. Firestone (1979), for example, argues that the 'privileged' position 'enjoyed' by children, including their protection from the labour market, is not freedom but rather a form of inequality and dependence. Child liberationists describe the 'separation' of the adult and child world as 'segregation'. They see it as an unwarranted and oppressive discrimination against children, which is accompanied and reinforced by a false ideology of 'childishness'. 'Childishness' which connotes vulnerability, frailty, and helplessness is not, they argue, a natural quality of children, but rather an ideological construct which helps to support the denial of their proper rights. Moreover, it is a self-confirming ideology, since, because of the way they are treated, children are denied the opportunity to show what they are really capable of.

Child liberationists argue that children are entitled to the same rights and privileges that adults enjoy, including rights to vote, work, own property, and rights to make sexual choices and make guardianship choices. The basis of their argument for children's rights is that even if a certain level or degree of competence is a justifiable criterion for the possession of rights, it is a mistake to judge *all* children as incompetent. For child liberationists, the assumption that all children are incompetent is a key ideological feature of modern conceptions of childhood. Their argument is that not all children are incompetent and therefore children as a whole should have the right to self-determination, just as adults do.

In opposition to the child liberationists stands what Archard (1993) calls 'the caretaker thesis'. It is this perspective, in essence, which provides the foundation for modern conceptions of childhood. The 'caretaker thesis' proposes that children should not be seen or treated as self-determining agents. Rather than children being free to make their own autonomous decisions, their 'caretakers' should make decisions for them. The paternalism which characterizes adult–child relations is justified because children themselves cannot make rational decisions and choices. The caretakers of children make decisions on behalf of children and choose in their best interests. They choose as the child itself would choose if it was a rational adult. The main concern, then, is to safeguard the interests of the future adult, which the child itself is unable to do.

Archard, in his book on children and rights, evaluates the competing perspectives of the child liberationists and the caretaker thesis. He argues against the child liberationists, saying that it is one thing to underestimate the capacities of children but something rather different to believe them equal to the capacities of adults. Archard's criticism of the caretaker thesis is the tendency to treat all children homogeneously, in that all children are viewed as incompetent. He suggests, then, that there are elements of truth in both approaches to the question of how children should be treated. It is mistaken to deny *all* children, on the grounds of incompetence, the right to self-determination. Clearly, infants and teenagers differ greatly from one another. Equally, though, it would be a mistake to grant self-determination to *all* children for precisely the same reasons. In conclusion, the attribution or withholding of rights for children is closely bound up with the ways in which the undeniable immaturity of young humans is interpreted and understood. Clearly, the immaturity of children in physical, psychological, and social terms is relevant to the understanding of power inequalities between children and adults. The problem is to decide *how much* emphasis should be placed on it in the organization of adult–child relations and the treatment of children as a social group (Prout and James 1990). In contemporary Western cultures, the immaturity of children is interpreted and understood in particular and specific ways and, consequently, a whole gamut of cultural practices and institutions are erected. This means that modern childhood in the West is organized more along the lines proposed by the 'caretakers' than by the 'liberationists'.

There are a number of recent developments in British society which can be interpreted as indicators that the liberationist perspective on childhood is gaining ground, however. For example, there has been the emergence of organizations which seek to listen to children's grievances, such as 'Childline'. Another sign that the powerlessness of children is beginning to be questioned is provided by the redefinition of corporal punishment as physical violence. In a court case in 1994, a childminder had to go to court to establish the right to smack children in her care (Jury and Dyer 1994). The 1989 Children Act can also be interpreted as an indication of a trend towards children's increased claims of 'personhood' as can the United Nations Convention on the Rights of the Child which the United Kingdom government agreed to be bound by in 1991.

THE UNITED NATIONS CONVENTION ON THE RIGHTS OF THE CHILD

The United Nations Convention on the Rights of the Child sets out the rights which all children and young people up to the age of 18 should have, wherever they live around the world. It says that children have three main rights which must be considered whenever any decision is being made about them, or any action is taken which affects them:

- *non-discrimination.* Article 2 of the Convention says that all the rights in the convention apply to all children equally whatever their race, sex, religion, language, disability, opinion, or family background.

- *best interests.* Article 3 says that when adults or organisations make decisions which affect children, they must always think first about what would be best for the child.

- *the child's view.* Article 12 says that children have the right to say what they think about anything which affects them. What children say must be listened to carefully. When courts or other official agencies are making decisions which affect children, they must listen to what the children want and feel.

The Convention also gives children civil and political rights and economic, social, cultural, and protective rights.

The British government agreed to be bound by the Convention in 1991. It is committed to support the Convention and to make it known to the public, although in entering certain 'reservations', it will not necessarily follow the Convention in every respect. Nevertheless, in 1994 and every five years after that, it will send the United Nations Committee on the Rights of the Child a report explaining how it is putting the Convention into practice.

Source: Children's Rights Development Unit 1993.

The Disappearance of Childhood?

If there are signs of an emerging trend towards reducing the powerlessness of children, this raises the issue of whether or not contemporary conceptions of childhood are undergoing change, and if there are shifts under way, what the extent of any changes are. Is it the case that the 'separation' of childhood from adulthood is breaking down? In this section, claims that childhood is disappearing are assessed. Alternative perspectives, including that which detects the 'globalization' of childhood, rather than its disappearance, are also considered.

The arguments made by Postman (1983) in his book *The Disappearance of Childhood* are in many ways representative of the notion that in modern industrialized societies, childhood is under threat. Postman's basic argument is that the idea of childhood is 'disappearing at a dazzling speed' and that the dividing line between childhood and adulthood is undergoing a process of rapid erosion. As evidence for this claim, Postman points to incidents of young criminals committing 'adult' crimes such as murder. He also highlights trends toward a similarity of clothing between adults and children, and the decline of children's games (games that are non-spectatored and non-supervised). According to Postman, this breakdown of the dividing line between children and adults has been accompanied by moves to give children the same rights as adults.

It is clear from the tone of Postman's argument that he regards the 'rapid erosion' of the dividing line between adults and children as regrettable and inappropriate. The factor which Postman identifies as the primary cause of the disappearance of childhood is revealed in the subtitle of his book: *How the dividing line between childhood and adulthood is being eroded by the electronic media.* The 'electronic medium' that Postman is particularly concerned with is television. For Postman, it is in television that we can see how and why the dividing line between adulthood and childhood is being eroded. He identifies three main ways in which television contributes to the disappearance of childhood. First, it requires no instruction on how to use it or watch it. Unlike reading, it is not necessary to learn how to watch television. Its image is available to everyone, regardless of age. Second, television does not make complex demands on behaviour. Third, it does not segregate its audience. For Postman, electronic forms of communication, such as television, find it impossible to withhold secrets and without secrets, he argues, there can be no such thing as childhood. Television and other related technologies eliminate the exclusive knowledge that belongs to adulthood. Television breaks down the 'quarantine period'. Through it, children are let into, are exposed to, the mysteries and secrets of adult life, including knowledge of sex, of death and illness, of violence, of consumerism, and of 'bad language' or swearing. Postman's concern is that, if children know the mysteries and secrets of adult life from the very start, how are they to be distinguished from adults? In summary, Postman argues that modern conceptions of childhood as 'separate' are a 'good thing' and its erosion and disappearance a 'bad thing'.

Television is to blame because its form and output eliminate differences which are necessary to sustain distinctions between childhood and adulthood.

In answer to the question, 'Is childhood disappearing?', Postman's response would be 'Yes it is, and it's a bad thing'. There are three other possible responses to the question of whether or not childhood is disappearing, and if it is disappearing, whether it is a 'good thing' or not. Wagg (1988) organizes the various possible positions in the debate in these ways and it is very useful to do so. In addition, then, to the 'Yes and it's a bad thing' position adopted by writers such as Postman, there is

- No, and it's a bad thing that it isn't disappearing
- No, and it's a good thing that it isn't disappearing
- Yes, it is disappearing and a good thing it is too

Most child liberationists fit into the 'No, and it's a bad thing that it isn't disappearing' category. For them, the way that modern childhood is organized is oppressive. They would argue that children continue to be made dependent, continue to be denied self-determination and autonomy, and so remain subject to authority relations in families, schools, and more generally. Hood-Williams (1990), although not necessarily a child liberationist, does argue against the disappearance of childhood thesis precisely along these lines. For Hood-Williams, despite the economic, political, and cultural changes of the post-war decades, childhood remains a firmly exclusionary status and children remain subject to the authority of adults. Whatever else has changed, he argues, children are still subject to the principle of obedience.

A slightly different way of stating that 'No, childhood is not disappearing and this is a bad thing' is the argument that childhood is, in fact, becoming 'internationalized' or 'globalized'. Boyden (1990) argues that there exists an 'official version' of childhood, which sees children as being demarcated from adults by a series of biological and psychological characteristics. As biological and psychological characteristics, they are, therefore, universally valid. The official version of childhood is reflected in the philosophies and practices of various international humanitarian and welfare agencies. The problem with it is that it is, in fact, a wholly Western, capitalist conception which tends to ignore the extreme cultural diversity that exists around the world. In spite of this, conceptions of childhood favoured by the Western nations have been exported and imposed on other nations and on other cultures. Ideas of childhood as 'separate', as based in the nuclear family, and as non-economically active are characteristic of Western models, yet they are being disseminated internationally. Boyden argues that global norms of childhood based on Western conceptions are spreading, a development which ignores the fact that different cultures hold different ideas about the competencies and capacities of children. From the point of view of Western-dominated welfare and humanitarian agencies, the presence of children on the street, absent from home, absent from school, are signals that are 'bad' and which require intervention and rectification. From the point of view of parents and children in these cultures, the activities of children outside the home and outside the school may be mechanisms of survival and, in preparing children for adult life, are part of the normal culture. To the extent, then, that Western conceptions of childhood are being exported to cultures where they may be inappropriate, far from disappearing, 'childhood' is spreading.

A third response to the question, 'Is childhood disappearing?' is 'No, it's not and that is good'. Here, evidence on the resilience of children's cultures can be cited. The Opies' studies on children's games, rhymes, and songs—the type of non-spectatored, non-supervised play activities feared by Postman to be disappearing—show a vibrant, independent, and creative cultural world inhabited by children, at least up until 1993 when their most recent research was published. Those taking up this position could also point to the various ways in which there still are differences between children and adults which, depending on one's perspective, can be seen as 'good' and 'valuable'. For example, the existence of children's play areas in supermarkets and whole television channels devoted to children's programming such as 'Nicolodean' can be interpreted and welcomed as cultural practices which re-establish the separation of childhood and adulthood in modern society.

The fourth position to the question 'Is childhood disappearing?' is 'Yes, it is and that's good'. Some child liberationists might interpret developments such as Childline and the Children Act as examples of moves towards an increase in children's 'personhood'. In many respects, those adopting this position in the debate would cite the same areas of change, such as children's exposure to the mysteries and secrets of the adult world, as those listed by Postman and viewed by him as regrettable. Wagg (1992), in his discussion of media, popular culture, and the politics of childhood, concludes that the logic of the evidence he has reviewed is that adult society is less protective and less concerned than in former times about the vulnerability of children as regards their exposure to sex, violence, or commerce. Moreover, he concludes that this change has been, on the whole, a beneficial one because the expressiveness, sensuality, and consumer role of the young have been acknowledged in the process.

There are, then a variety of responses to the question of whether or not childhood, or rather modern forms of childhood, are 'disappearing'. Which response is favoured depends on which area or aspect of children's lives is focused upon. Whilst it may be true that television does bring sex, violence, and commerce into children's lives, they remain subject to the authority of adults. Despite developments such as the Children Act 1989, children do not have equal rights with adults. Childhood still takes place primarily in family and educational settings. Arguably, schooling and dependency have become ever more characteristic features of childhood, as 'children' now remain, in the context of limited employment opportunities, in school, education, or training until they are 18 years old. Consequently, young people remain dependent upon parental support for much longer than previously, leading commentators to argue that transitions to adulthood have become prolonged (see Chapter Four).

Whilst the duration of education and training of young people has lengthened, increasing pressures caused by 'qualification inflation' mean that childhood has become a stage characterized by the intensive 'chasing of credentials'. The introduction of the National Curriculum and testing at ages 7, 11, and 14 can be interpreted as an attempt to encourage specified educational achievements within childhood. As a result, in educational achievement terms at least, childhood is becoming ever more tightly defined into stages.

Although children's spatial range may be extensive in the sense of the availability of television (including satellite stations), telephone, and computer networks, parental concerns about road accidents and 'danger from strangers' has meant increased restrictions on their actual freedom of movement (Figure 3.3). More generally, there remain strongly voiced concerns over children in terms of standards of behaviour and discipline and their exposure to sex and violence. Often, the issues of behaviour and discipline are linked to exposure to sex and violence, so that delinquent and criminal activities of children are interpreted as a consequence of their viewing of so-called 'video nasties'.

To these extents then, childhood as 'separateness' largely remains the dominant conceptualization in modern Britain. Ultimately, it is difficult to assess the disappearance of childhood thesis because of seemingly contradictory trends and a lack of real evidence about childhood itself, as it is experienced and created by children themselves. One development which may impinge on the 'disappearance' of childhood

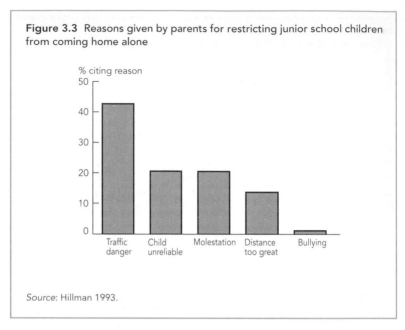

Figure 3.3 Reasons given by parents for restricting junior school children from coming home alone

Source: Hillman 1993.

thesis is the changing demographic trends in the numbers of children. As detailed in Chapter One, the number of children under 16 is projected to rise by about 5 per cent between 1992 and 2002, and thereafter to fall slowly until 2020. Throughout the twentieth century, the decrease in fertility and increased longevity have resulted in a changed age structure, so that younger people as a percentage of the total population has declined. As Qvortrup (1990) suggests such changes mean that a new analysis is needed of the position of children and the status of childhood. With relatively fewer children around, it may be that the strength of their potential representation for societal resources will diminish, as the number of adults with everyday interests in children's lives is reduced. Qvortrup also points to trends in fertility whereby women are having fewer children and at later ages, so that less of their lives is taken up with childrearing. Qvortrup's conclusion is that the cultural climate of Western societies is bound to change as children are reduced as a proportion of the population. Whether children will, via their relative scarcity value, become more or less powerful, more or less valuable as a result of the demographic changes are open questions. Future research will have to detect whether children become more deeply embedded in constricting conceptualizations of childhood as a consequence of their relative scarcity, or whether they will, in fact, find it easier to escape from childhood.

Further Reading

The most important recent texts are those edited by Chisholm (1990) and James and Prout (1990). A useful source of a cross-cultural and historical evidence is Hoyles (1979). Fyfe (1989) provides information on children and work around the world. Pollard (1987) reports on children in their primary schools, often using their own accounts and explanations. Opie's (1993) recent book reports on children's play up to the 1980s.

Chapter Four

Youth

The concept of youth, like that of childhood, is a way of understanding the 'growing up' stage of the life course. Whilst children have tended to be viewed in terms of the adults they will eventually become, youth are viewed, simultaneously, in terms of what they no longer are (children) *and* what they nearly are (adults). As with all other stages of the life course, assigning precise chronological ages to the beginning and end of youth is extremely problematical. In modern Britain, youth might be said to correspond with the teenage years of a person's life. However, even such a broad linking of chronological ages to youth as a stage is far from satisfactory, particularly given the changes in young people's lives in recent decades. As this chapter will show, such changes mean that adulthood, on some criteria, is not seen to start until the age of 26. Rather than linking definitions of youth to a particular chronological age range, youth is best understood as a position between childhood and adulthood, and characterized as a stage of *transition* from the one to the other. In modern Britain, youth is a key period of transition between the dependent and powerless state of childhood and the independent, autonomous, and relatively powerful stage of adulthood. If childhood is located in the school and adulthood in employment, then youth sees the beginnings of withdrawal from compulsory full-time education and the entry into employment. If childhood takes place in the family of *origin*, with parents and siblings, and adulthood takes place in families of *destination*, with sexual partners and offspring (or some other form of independent household), then youth marks the beginnings of the transition between the two (Figure 4.1). The education to employment transition and the family of origin to family of destination transition are highlighted here as the two key components in the transition from childhood to adulthood which the concept of youth encapsulates. Youth, then, is not childhood nor adulthood, but is the life course stage positioned in between.

In British sociology, youth has been studied mainly in terms of youth

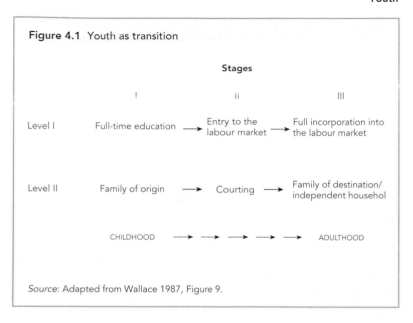

Figure 4.1 Youth as transition

Stages

	I		II		III
Level I	Full-time education	→	Entry to the labour market	→	Full incorporation into the labour market
Level II	Family of origin	→	Courting	→	Family of destination/ independent househol

CHILDHOOD → → → → → ADULTHOOD

Source: Adapted from Wallace 1987, Figure 9.

cultures and in terms of the school to work transition. This chapter draws on evidence from both traditions of youth research to provide an account of the changes that have occurred in young people's experiences within youth in recent decades. The chapter illustrates that the different ways in which youth in Britain has been studied are tightly bound up with both the changing history of sociology and the changing history of society. Developments in sociology as a discipline, particularly the influence of functionalist perspectives, and their subsequent critique, and the more recent concern with young people within their family context, are evident in the changed concerns and focus of youth research in the post-war period. The contrasting economic and political conditions during this period can also be seen to have greatly influenced both the experiences of young people themselves and the way sociologists have studied them.

Beginning with a brief sketch of youth in modern Britain, this chapter then examines the historical emergence of youth in European societies. The variability of youth as a socially constructed life course stage is further emphasized via reference to cross-cultural evidence. The main focus of the chapter is the changing meanings of, and experiences within, youth as a life course stage in post-war Britain to the present day. Coffield (1987) characterizes the changes during this period as a shift from the 'celebration' to the 'marginalization' of youth. The chapter assesses the implications of such a shift for young people's opportunities and experiences, particularly in terms of their attainment of 'adulthood'.

Youth in Modern Britain

An important argument made by sociologists of age is that physiological aspects of growing up and growing older are less important than the ways in which various societies at various times interpret, understand, and attach significance to physiological ageing. This argument is particularly relevant to the study of the transition from childhood to adulthood, for there are clear physiological differences between 'children' and 'adults'. *Puberty* refers to the various physiological changes that differentiate adults from children, changes that accompany and include the development of reproductive capacities (see box opposite). Puberty is a universal phenomenon, occurring across cultures and across historical time. However, the beginning of puberty varies in terms of the chronological age at its onset. The physiology of human beings is greatly affected by cultural factors, including diet and stress (Field and Field 1980), and therefore precisely when puberty begins varies between individuals, across cultures and over time. In modern Britain, puberty occurs at around the age of 12, whilst in pre-industrial times, the physical changes associated with puberty occurred up to three or four years later (Gillis 1974). In physiological terms, adulthood can be said to be achieved with puberty. However, as the section on the history of youth will show, in pre-industrial Europe, people remained 'youths' long after they experienced puberty, even if this did occur as late as age 16. In modern Britain, with puberty generally taking place during the early teenage years, young people are not regarded or treated as adults merely because their bodies have matured. Physical maturity, then, does not automatically bring social maturity, at least not in modern Britain, or in its pre-industrial past. In other cultural traditions, though, greater significance may sometimes be attached to puberty as a sign of reaching adulthood (see below).

Although experiencing puberty may not qualify children for entry into the adult world, the bodily changes it brings about are important for modern conceptualizations of youth as a stage of transition between childhood and adulthood. James (1986) argues that the bodies of young people are a major definitional criterion for marking adolescence. In

PUBERTY

The physiological changes which constitute puberty have been classified as follows:

• acceleration and then deceleration of skeletal growth
• altered body composition as a result of skeletal and muscular growth, together with changes in the quantity and distribution of fat
• development of the circulatory and respiratory systems leading to increased strength and endurance
• development of the gonads, reproductive organs, and secondary sexual characteristics
• a combination of factors which modulates the activity of those nervous and endocrine elements which initiate and co-ordinate all of these changes

Source: Katchadourian 1978.

modern Britain, the changing size, shape, and functioning of young people's bodies caused by puberty are important 'visual images' which indicate their changing status. The 'folk model' of adolescence thus interprets changes in attitudes and temperament as outward manifestations of the inward bodily changes occurring with the onset of puberty (James 1986). Physical changes link with psychological changes and social changes in the lives of young people undergoing the transition to adulthood, so that the folk model conceptualization is of youth as a time of stress, turmoil, and change. It is also seen as a time of coming to terms with these changes, via the exploration of values and ideas, of one's self and one's place in the world.

That the physiological onset of maturity is not, in modern Britain, a passport to *social* maturity as adults is evident from the withholding of adult rights and responsibilities until several years *after* most young people have experienced puberty. Table 4.1 lists the various chronological ages at which young people attain adult rights and responsibilities. In modern Britain, the transition from childhood to adulthood, referred to as youth, can be seen as a lengthy process of gradual and incremental inclusion into independent adulthood (Hutson and Jenkins 1989). Expectations concerning the amount of independence young people should have from their families varies, though, according to the cultural origins of their parents. A study by Brannen *et al.* (1994) found that whilst the United Kingdom-born parents of young people saw it as 'normal' for their sons and daughters to become progressively more

Table 4.1 Official ages of adulthood in modern Britain

Age	Context
10	Age of criminal responsibility (8 in Scotland)
13	Minimum age for employment
14	Own an air rifle
	Pay the adult fare on public transport
16	Leave school
	(Heterosexual) Age of consent to sexual intercourse
	Buy cigarettes
	Marry with parental consent
	Hold a licence to drive a moped
	Eligible for full-time employment
17	Hold a licence to drive a car
18	Vote in elections
	Buy alcohol
	Watch films and videos classified as '18'
	(Homosexual) Age of consent[a]
	Marry without parental consent
25	Adult levels of Income Support
26	Adult in housing benefit rules

[a] In February 1994, the homosexual age of consent was lowered to 18 following a vote in the House of Commons.

Sources: Wagg 1988, Table 1; Jones and Wallace 1992, Table 5.1.

independent, those parents born outside the United Kingdom generally did not see youth as a time of increasing separation from the household. Rather, the transition to adulthood was regarded, especially by those parents born and raised in Asian and Middle Eastern countries, as entailing a greater responsibility toward others in the household and kinship group.

Official criteria of adulthood, such as those listed in Table 4.1, often do not coincide. Whether a youth is an adult is variable and dependent upon the specific context: whether it is buying cigarettes, drinking alcohol, driving a car, having sexual intercourse (and with whom), or voting in a national election. In some of these situations, young persons are officially adults and thus legally able to participate on the basis of their chronological age, whilst in others, at the same chronological age, they are not.

The popular characterization of youth as a period of stress and turmoil is perhaps understandable given that young people have the physical capacities to, say, enjoy sex, make a baby, drive a car, or engage in full-time employment, long before they are socially or legally permitted to. Official criteria of adulthood are important, even if they lack consistency, but of far greater significance for sociologists are the markers of adulthood evident in cultural practices. Various sociologists have suggested the following as important criteria of adulthood in modern Britain:

- physical maturity, via puberty
- leaving full-time education
- entering employment and earning a wage
- leaving the parental home
- setting up an independent home
- family formation, via sexual partnerships and parenthood
- independence as a consumer
- legal recognition of citizenship

These events, activities, and behaviours can be taken as indicators of what being an adult seems to be in modern British cultural practices. The concept of 'adulthood' is discussed more fully in Chapter Five, whilst the position and experiences of young people in modern Britain in relation to some of these markers of adulthood are examined shortly, following sections which draw historical and cross-cultural comparisons on youth as the transition from childhood to adulthood.

Youth in History

Aries's 'invention of childhood' thesis suggests that pre-industrial European societies accepted children into the adult world once they had reached the age of 5 or thereabouts. The implication is that, at this time, the existence of any intermediate stage was not recognized. However, Gillis (1974) argues that pre-industrial societies did recognize and institutionalize a stage of life that was different from childhood and adulthood. Pre-industrial conceptions of youth do not, though, correspond with modern meanings or to its chronological markers.

In pre-industrial society, what was commonly referred to as 'youth' was a very long transition period, lasting from about the age of 7 to the age at marriage, an event which usually occurred in the mid to late twenties. According to Gillis, the onset of youth as a stage began when children, under the apprenticeship system, left their families and lived in other households as servants or apprentices to a trade. In pre-industrial societies, then, youth was a stage characterized by a gradually more extensive detachment from the family of origin, and a state of semi-dependence in the household of those to whom they were apprenticed. This semi-dependent status continued until complete independence, at marriage (Gillis 1974: 2). The lack of differentiation made between younger and older individuals within youth was largely a consequence of the fact that neither work nor education was sharply age-graded. Gillis argues that puberty itself did not hold much significance as a marker, because children were accustomed to assuming adult sex roles. Moreover, the attainment of puberty was not signified by a change in clothing or other such external indicator (1974: 6).

Processes of industrialization and urbanization transformed the economic and social lives of youth 'tying young workers closer to their families and neighbourhoods' (Gillis 1974: 56). Young people began to stay home with their families and left only a short time before setting up their own households. As the nineteenth century progressed, the younger age group of youth became increasingly subject to parental and other institutional controls, via their exclusion from the labour market and the extension of formal schooling. From 1900 onwards, Gillis argues, a more modern conceptualization of youth came into being, one which was applied to the 'teenaged'. 'Social and psychological theories of the instability and vulnerability of the age-group justified a deluge of protective legislation which, by 1914, had radically curbed its independence' (Gillis 1974: 133). Organizations such as the Scouts were founded and special prisons, courts, employment, and welfare agencies were set up. These developments signalled society's recognition, particularly for males, of youth as a life course stage in the modern world, one that should be free from cares and responsibilities (1974: 182) but that was nevertheless vulnerable to deviance unless carefully protected (1974: 171).

Although not clearly apparent in the above summary, Gillis does pay attention to social class in his analysis of the history of youth. He describes the emergence of separate working-class and middle-class 'traditions of youth', in the form of gang behaviour, particularly from the eighteenth century onwards. Gillis also argues that the modern conceptualization of youth, focused around the teenage years as a period of vulnerability and instability, was a largely middle-class creation, subsequently extended to include the 'teenaged' of all social classes.

Clearly, the history of childhood and the history of youth are closely intertwined and changes since medieval times in the one have had ramifications for the other. From ages 7 to the late twenties being a semi-dependent stage, characterized by residential independence from family of origin and a worker-like status, the stage of life referred to as youth has, over time, become compressed. Those at the bottom age range of 'traditional' youth became enveloped in the modern conception of childhood, whilst the others had, by the early twentieth century, themselves been drawn into a more fully dependent status within their families of origin and within the formal education system.

Childhood to Adulthood Transitions: a Cross-Cultural Perspective

Through a comparison of the ways in which other societies manage and mark the transition from childhood to adulthood, the particular features of youth as a stage in the life course in modern Britain are revealed. This section presents evidence from cultures which mark the transition from childhood to adulthood, via acts or ceremonies of initiation, rituals which are largely absent from modern Britain, and many other industrialized cultures (Hockey and James 1993). In societies where the separation of the world of childhood and the world of adulthood is less marked than in contemporary Britain, transition from the one to the other may be easier to complete and take a shorter amount of time.

In some cultures, the transition to adulthood is achieved with the completion of a single act. Langley (1979) studied initiation rituals amongst the Nandi people of Kenya and argued that the 'supremely important' moment in the life of a youth is the moment of his circumcision. 'By means of the flick of the knife at the climax of a long ritual process, boyhood becomes a thing of the past and manhood is entered' (1979: 19). Such incisive moments of transition from the status of child to adult are often accompanied by lengthy ritual processes. According to a study by Richards, the *Chisunga* ceremony of the Bemba people of Zambia secures the 'transition from a calm but unproductive girlhood to a potentially dangerous but fertile womanhood' (1982: 125). The ceremony takes place after a girl has had her first period and after this event has itself been marked by a separate 'puberty rite'. The puberty rite may involve ceremonial washing of the girl and isolation indoors before her return to the community. The girl then waits until it is convenient for her *Chisunga* ceremony to begin. This ceremony is composed of many individual rituals, including the physical testing of the girl through various ordeals, her social isolation as a form of ritual separation and the singing of ritual songs. The ceremony lasts for over a month and ends with the girl's change of status being marked by the end of her social isolation. The girl is bathed, dressed in new clothes, brought out of the hut, and placed on a new mat outside its door. The girl sits in silence in front of the villagers, who throw small presents on to the mat. The *Chisunga* prepares girls for marriage, by teaching them the 'secrets' of Bemba women, by making them 'grow', and by making them 'women'. At the end of the ceremony, girls are considered ready for marriage and, often, a marriage ceremony immediately follows (Richards 1982).

Evidence from other cultures shows that the movement from childhood to adulthood can be accomplished through initiation ceremonies, rituals which transform an individuals' status from that of a child to an adult. In modern Britain, youth as a stage in the transition between childhood and adulthood has few ritual markers and the moment of transition to adulthood is much less precise.

Young People in Britain: 1945 to the Present

The period from the post-war decades up to the 1980s has been characterized by Coffield (1987) as one which saw a change from the 'celebration' to the 'marginalization' of youth. This section charts the changing fortunes of young people in the post-war period and considers the implications of the changes for the completion of their transition to adulthood.

The 'Celebration' of Youth: the 1950s to 1960s

The decades of the 1950s and 1960s were characterized by a series of distinctive youth cultures. During these decades, many commentators, populist and academic alike, believed that age had become the most pre-eminent form of social division and source of social conflict. The youth cultures of the period were regarded as highly visible manifestations of the emergence of age as a basis for social differentiation. What was the background to the emergence of the distinctive youth cultures? What form did they take? Did age supersede class as the major basis of social division and social conflict? These are some of the issues discussed in this account of the experiences of young people in the immediate post-war decades. The variety of ways in which sociologists have

tried to explain the phenomenon of youth culture are also considered.

A starting-point for the analysis of the youth cultures of the 1950s and
1960s is Abrams's (1959) paper on the 'teenage consumer'. Abrams
presents figures which show that between 1938 and 1958, the real earnings of young people increased by over 50 per cent. This rate of increase
was double that of adult earnings over the same period. In his paper,
Abrams also presents figures which show that teenage spending in the
late 1950s made up a significant proportion of total spending on leisure
goods and services. The teenager was an important consumer of
records and stereo equipment, bicycles, mopeds, motorcycles, and cosmetics and accounted for over one quarter of cinema admissions. Frith
(1984) argues that Abrams's research was important because it
described a new and distinctive form of youth behaviour.

As a consumer group, young people were distinguished from other age groups
not by their 'bad' behaviour, but simply in terms of their market choices, and it
was these choices that revealed a new 'teenage culture'. This culture was defined
in terms of leisure and leisure goods—coffee and milk bars, fashion clothes and
hair styles, cosmetics, rock'n'roll records, films and magazines, scooters and
motorbikes, dancing and dance halls. (Frith 1984: 9)

Youth cultures of the 1950s and 1960s were marked by the appearance of a series of highly stylized, highly public expressions of youthful
identity. There were the Teddy Boys, the Mods, the rockers, each with a
distinctive style of dress and a distinctive style of music. These were
mainly white, working-class, male youth cultures which Brake (1985)
describes as being part-time, in that they were participated in out of
work time. Later, in the 1960s, there were the more middle-class youth
cultures, such as the beatniks, the hippies, and the student radicals.
Brake argues that these middle-class 'counter-cultures' had a more
complete influence over a participant's life-style, so that there was a
fusion between work and leisure time. Again, these were white and
male-dominated youth cultures. The various youth cultures of this
period have been fully described and analysed by Brake (1985) and
Frith (1984), amongst others.

It was the particular social and economic context of the 1950s and
1960s which gave rise to the distinctive youth cultures in the immediate
post-war period and which, more generally, shaped the experiences of
young people in those decades. A variety of factors can be highlighted,
including the increase in young people as a proportion of the total population, a demographic change which can be expected to have resulted
in altered perceptions about the relative importance of young people,

in both a quantitative and qualitative sense. Other factors include the legacy of the Second World War, that is, of a disruption of previously established patterns of social behaviour and social experience more generally. This allowed a gap for new standards and new experiences to take root. Probably the most important factor in shaping the experiences of young people in the 1950s and 1960s was the change in the economic structure during this period. The post-war decades were those of the 'you have never had it so good' rhetoric and characterized by full employment and the importing of labour from the countries of the commonwealth. These were the decades of affluence, and as Abrams's (1959) analysis shows, young people benefited greatly in terms of their increase in real earnings. Young people could leave school at 15, and the economic climate was such that gaining a job was straightforward. At a stage in their life when they were unburdened by adult responsibilities and dependants, their spending was devoted to 'leisure and pleasure', to the pleasure of not being grown up and not having adult responsibilities (Frith 1984).

Various commentators have argued that in the post-war decades, youth began to be viewed as a metaphor for the wider social changes that were taking place. Young people were regarded as being at the vanguard of social change (Clarke *et al.* 1976), and were the embodiment of freedom, of good times, a way of defining an ideal way of life. This way of looking at youth became even more firmly entrenched with the emergence of the middle-class 'counter-cultures' of the 1960s. According to Murdock and McCron (1976), youth was seen as becoming 'a generation for itself' with a distinctive consciousness and style. The 'hippies' were the 'advanced guard', rehearsing possible cultural solutions to the central life problems posed by post-war affluent society.

For many at the time, the youth cultures of the post-war decades were evidence that differences based on age had become more important and more fundamental than differences based on social class. Roszak (1970) argued that what he saw as the 'rivalry' between young people and adults in Western societies in the 1960s was unique and was the most important source of radical dissent and cultural innovation. He writes, 'For better or for worse, most of what is presently happening that is new, provocative, and engaging, in politics, education, the arts, social relations (love, courtship, family, community) is the creation, either of youth, or those who address themselves primarily to the young' (Roszak 1970: 2).

The idea that age had become the most important basis of social differentiation was, in part, reflected in functionalist analyses of youth culture. For Parsons (1954*a*; 1954*b*) and Eisenstadt (1956), age differentiation is of great importance for the functioning of the social system and for the individual personality (see Chapter Two). Eisenstadt puts forward an account of the *functions* of youth cultures for both society and the individual young person. He argues that, as part of the process of socialization into mature adult societal membership, young people must rid themselves of patterns of behaviour enacted with parents or other adult kin. In pre-modern societies, this transfer of identification and solidarity away from the family to society is a relatively smooth process. The individual is able to attain adult status within the social system through patterns of behaviour acquired within the family. In modern societies, though, the individual needs to learn to act according to universalistic and generalized standards, rather than to the particularistic and ascriptive standards of family life. As a consequence, young people in modern societies develop the need for a new kind of interaction which makes the transfer of identification and solidarity easier. The individual is led to seek relationships which provide emotional security but at the same time allow him or her to act according to criteria other than those which predominate in family and kinship groups. According to Eisenstadt relationships with 'age mates' fulfil these needs. Youth groups are therefore partly defensive against future adult roles and partly oriented toward them (Eisenstadt 1956). Talcott Parsons similarly argues that youth cultures have the function of easing the process of adjustment from childhood to adulthood. Young people have to leave the emotional dependency of childhood in preparation for their adult relationships with members of the opposite sex and for their occupational roles. Whilst in one sense, youth cultures prepare young people for adulthood, at the same time they 'repudiate an interest in adult things', being characterized by irresponsibility, pleasure seeking, and a concern with having a good time (Parsons 1954*a*; 1954*b*).

Functionalist accounts refer to youth cultures in a uniform undifferentiated way, probably with American, urban, white, middle-class males as their model. In criticism of this universalism, the British cultural studies perspective argues that youth is differentiated by social class. In so doing, these Marxist theorists directly contradict claims that age had begun to matter more than social class in modern Britain (Clarke *et al.* 1976). The cultural studies perspective argues that youth cultures 'win space' for young people; culturally, spatially, and timewise. They are described as a collective response by young people to their position in a class society, particularly by working-class boys. The stylized form of youth cultures is an indication that they are also attempts at 'symbolic solutions' to the concrete problems of young people's position in a class society. The Teddy Boy expropriation of upper-class Edwardian-style clothes, for example, can be interpreted as a symbolic solution to the reality of manual unskilled careers and life chances (Clarke *et al.* 1976). Middle-class youth cultures of the 1960s were similarly interpreted in terms of the class specificity of their origin and form. Frith summarizes the argument of the cultural studies perspective like this: 'Youth groups use their own area of power—their free time—to make a gesture against their lot. Their material situation is at one level accepted . . . but, at another level, rejected—deviant styles symbolize a refusal to accept dominant accounts of their position' (1984: 47).

The cultural studies perspective dominated research on young people in Britain in the 1970s and early 1980s (Chisholm 1990). It has been heavily criticized especially for its concentration on male youth (McRobbie and Garber 1976) and for focusing on the activities of 'spectacular' rather than 'ordinary' youth (see Frith 1984 for overview of critiques). The debates addressed by the cultural studies perspective on youth, as well as the critiques of it, underline the necessity of recognizing that age must be understood as a variable which acts in articulation with *other* social variables, particularly social class, gender, race, and ethnicity. Young people, like other age groups, are not just *young* people: they are 'classed', 'raced', and 'gendered' young people.

Both functionalist and cultural studies perspectives argue that youth is a key period of transition and that youth cultures arise as a 'coping strategy' for young people at this key stage of the life course. Cultural studies perspectives differ from functionalist perspectives in that they emphasize that youth cultural responses are differentiated by social class. In turn, critics of the cultural studies perspective argue that youth cultures are also differentiated by gender, race, and ethnicity. Brake (1985) argues further that the experiences of youth are also shaped by *historical* contexts. Brake suggests that each cohort of young people has to 'work out' or 'work through' the problems of transition to adulthood and the problems of their social class position within new historical contexts. Young people's location in historical time means that they are likely to experience problems which arise from their social class position and their stage in life course position *differently*, both to those who have gone before them and to those who will come after them. In this way, then, it is possible to explain the ways in which stage in life course and location in historical time can interact with class and other variables to give rise to historically distinctive youth cultures.

Much of the sociological research on youth has been in terms of the leisure activities of young people and this can be regarded as a limitation (Frith 1984). However, there is a long-established tradition in British sociology of researching the school-to-work transition of young people, a tradition which the dominance of the cultural studies perspective for a time acted to obscure (Chisholm 1990). The 1950s and 1960s cohorts of young people entered the labour market during a time of relative affluence and full employment. As Abrams's (1959) analysis shows, these young people benefited greatly in terms of increased wages. Coffield (1987) describes this period as the 'Golden Age' of youth. What do studies of the school to work transition show about young people's experiences in this respect?

Carter (1962) carried out a study of 200 school leavers in 1959. He found that one-half of the sample obtained jobs before they left school. Of those that had not, half of the boys and two-thirds of the girls had found work within a fortnight of leaving school. Less than ten girls and ten boys had not found work within four weeks of leaving school. Carter comments, however, that 'some of these had not tried very hard' to find work (1962: 162). A year after leaving school, only one boy was without a job, and no girls were unemployed, although two were 'not working' (one because of marriage). Carter notes the lack of difficulty in finding jobs due to there being no overall shortage of employment. Over a third of the young people studied in 1959 by Carter were found to have changed their job during their first year of employment. Reasons for job changing included general dissatisfaction with the job, dissatisfaction with future prospects in the job, and dissatisfaction with wage levels. After leaving a job, few young people experienced periods of unemployment of more than a week, if they did so at all (Carter 1962).

The buoyancy of the job market for young people in the 1950s and 1960s is also confirmed by Maizels's (1970) slightly later study, of young people and the transition from school to work in 1965. Maizels studied 330 boys and girls aged 15 to 18 and found that over half the sample had obtained their first jobs whilst still at school, the other half within the first few weeks of leaving school. Maizels found that over half of the boys and around two-thirds of the girls were successful in obtaining the first job for which they had applied. She writes that 'most school leavers, could, therefore, be assumed to have had little difficulty in finding their first employment' (1970: 117).

In the 1950s and 1960s there is no doubt that a variety of factors acted in combination to create a historical context which presented young people with unique experiences and which raised the profile of age as a basis of social differentiation and simultaneously reduced the profile of class. The youth cultures of the 1950s and 1960s were in many ways unique. They were stylistically unique, they were specific responses to particular processes of social and economic change and they were responses made by people at a particular and specific stage of the life course. Furthermore, patterns of household and family formation amongst young people changed during the post-war decades, as evidenced by the sixfold increase in first marriage rates for teenagers between the end of the Second World War and the early 1970s (Coleman 1988). At the turn of the century (when marriage was allowed at ages 14 for males and 12 for females), the average age at marriage was 26.4 years for men and 25.3 years for women. The gradual trend towards earlier ages at marriage throughout the first part of the twentieth century was accelerated in the immediate post-war decades, so that in the mid to late 1960s, males were on average aged 23.8 years, and females 21.7 years, at their marriage (OPCS 1977). This was also the period when an important official marker of adulthood changed. In 1969 the legal age of majority was lowered from 21 years to 18 years, following the recommendations of the 1967 Latey Committee.

Arguments about the ascendancy of age and the descendency of class, then, have to be understood in the social, economic, and political contexts of the time. In the face of young people's affluence, their younger ages at marriage, and their younger age of legal majority, it is easy to see why age was thought to be of increasing social significance. In the context of affluence, consensus politics, and the apparent *embourgoisement* of the working class (Clarke *et al.* 1976), it is not surprising that the relevance of class was seen to be in decline. However, class did not disappear as a source of social conflict and social identity in the immediate post-war decades, as the 'rediscovery' of poverty in the 1960s underlined. Cultural studies perspectives showed youth cultures to be differentiated by class, and the *embourgoisement* thesis was largely refuted. Arguments concerning the increased importance of age relative to class, in any case, soon came to be overtaken by events. The 1970s recessions and the decline in youth employment meant that the whole context of the argument had altered. Rather than attention being focused on youth in terms of affluence, culture, and leisure, sociological attention shifted to youth in terms of *unemployment*.

The 'Marginalization' of Youth: the 1980s to the Present

Griffin writes that, by the 1980s, youth research was compelled to 'consider what happens when the transition from school to work becomes a move from the classroom to the dole queue' (1987: 86). Earlier in this chapter, it was suggested that youth is best understood as a period of transition, comprising of two main components: the transition from education to the labour market and the transition from family of origin to family of destination, or to some other form of independent household. Much of the sociological research on young people since the 1980s, under the influence of life course perspectives, has been concerned with the impact of mass youth unemployment upon these two components of the transition to adulthood and the consequences for the attainment of adult status and adult identities. Before examining the findings of this body of research on young people's transition to adulthood, it is first necessary to detail the ways in which young people's experiences in the labour market have changed since the late 1970s.

Table 4.2 Educational and economic activities of 16–18 year olds, Great Britain, 1976–1990 (%)

	1976	1986	1990
Full-time education	27	31	36
In employment	65	43	} 49
Unemployed	8	15	
YOP and YTS	—	10	15

Source: Central Statistical Office 1994a.

The most notable change in the labour market experiences of young people since the mid to late 1970s has been the marked decline in their levels of employment. In 1976, 65 per cent of 16–18-year-olds were in employment. A decade later, with overall numbers of 16–18-year-olds having increased, less than half (43 per cent) of this age group were in employment (Table 4.2). This decline in levels of employment amongst young people is the consequence of a combination of demand and supply factors. On the demand side, the recessions of the 1970s and 1980s hit young workers particularly hard. Young workers lack skills and experience and are therefore less productive and cost effective as employees. Also on the demand side, structural shifts in the economy have seen the decline of traditional heavy industries and the manufacturing sector. This has meant a reduction in the number of opportunities in the lower manual segment of the labour market, an important entry point for young workers (Ashton, Maguire, and Garland 1982). The expansion of the service sector has not been sufficient to compensate for the loss of jobs in traditional industries. On the supply side, young people entering the labour market in the late 1970s and throughout the 1980s were part of a relatively large cohort. This meant that there were more young people chasing fewer jobs. Another supply-side factor which may have impacted upon levels of employment amongst young people is the increase in labour market participation rates by married women. Since the majority of women work in low-paid jobs which are regarded as low skilled, they are often in direct competition with young people for this type of employment.

Whatever the exact combination of reasons for the decline in levels of youth employment, it is clear that young people entering the labour market in the 1980s faced a very different set of opportunities to those young people studied by Carter (1962) and Maizels (1970). The main features of the changes in the labour market experiences of young people are summarized in the box opposite. One consequence of the decline in youth employment has been an increase in youth *unemployment*. Data from the Labour Force Survey show that in 1977, 10 per cent of 16–19-year-old and 7.5 per cent of 20–4-year-old males were unemployed. The figures for (non-married) females are 9.5 per cent and 7 per cent respectively. By 1985, 20 per cent of 16–19-year-old and 17 per cent of 20–4-year-old males were unemployed. The figures for (non-married) females are 18 per cent and 12 per cent respectively. By 1991, although rates of unemployment had come down a little, they still remained higher than in the 1970s. In 1991, 16 per cent of 16–19-year-old and 15 per cent of 20–4-year-old males were unemployed. The figures for (non-married) females show a similar pattern at 12 per cent and 9 per cent respectively (OPCS 1980; 1987; 1992).

A second consequence of the decline in levels of youth employment is that increasing numbers of young people are remaining in full-time education. In 1976, only 27 per cent of 16–18-year-olds were in full-time education. By 1986, this had increased to 31 per cent and, in 1990, had reached 36 per cent (Table 4.2). Jones and Wallace (1992) argue that 'student' has become an important intermediate status for increasing numbers of young people. (It is important to recognize, though, that the level of courses studied, institutions attended and the amount of financial support received vary greatly.) Jones and Wallace describe the status of student as a subordinate one, without adult autonomy, income, or responsibilities. It is one of the ways in which young people's transition to economic independence has become delayed, in comparison to the 1950s and 1960s.

A third area of change is that training schemes have become an insti-tutionalized part of many young people's early labour market experi-

---

MAIN FEATURES OF CHANGES IN YOUNG PEOPLE'S LABOUR
MARKET EXPERIENCES

* decline in levels of employment
* increase in levels of unemployment
* increase in post-16 participation rates in education
* increase in participation in training schemes
* reduction in wages
* loss of apprenticeships
* increase in part-time and casual work
* abolition of Wages Councils
* withdrawal of employment protection
* erosion in entitlements to social security benefits, including supplementary benefit or Income Support, housing assistance and student grants

Sources: Jones and Wallace 1992; Pilcher and Williamson 1988.

---

ences: prior to the 1970s such schemes did not exist (Table 4.2). Training schemes aimed at young people have taken a variety of forms since they were first introduced. For young people under the age of 18, the emphasis has been on training and the imparting of vocational skills, as in the two-year employer-based Youth Training Scheme (YTS). Trainees are paid an allowance, rather than a wage, and there is no guarantee of a job at the end of the period of training. A 1987 survey by the Manpower Services Commission found that around half of YTS trainees went on to full-time employment, with well over one-quarter returning to unemployment (Pilcher and Williamson 1988).

These substantive changes in the form of the youth labour market have both contributed to and been accompanied by changes in its content. Young workers in the 1950s and 1960s enjoyed significant increases in their wages relative to those of adults. By the 1970s and 1980s, though, a combination of factors exerted a downward pressure on wages earned by young people. 'Flexible' working, in the form of part-time, temporary, and casual work has increasingly become a feature of young people's labour market experiences, and are part of an overall decline in the quality of employment available to young people (see box above).

The changes in young people's post-16 education to the labour market transition experiences have not, of course, impacted upon them in a uniform way. The age, social class, gender, and ethnicity of a young person have been shown to influence the routes taken in the transition from education to the labour market. The possession of educational qualifications, region of the country, vibrancy of the local labour market and, in Northern Ireland especially, religion are further factors which influence the transition routes of young people.

The various changes in young people's experience of the transition from education to employment and in their early labour market experiences have led sociologists to describe transition routes to adulthood as having become 'broken', 'collapsed', or, less dramatically, 'prolonged'. Such descriptions, however, arise from an assumption that there previously existed 'normal' or even 'natural' transition routes for young people. In reality, transition routes from childhood to adulthood are variable and change over historical time, as Gillis (1974) shows. Clearly, the education to employment transition *has* changed over the last decade or so and the contrast with the 1950s and 1960s is quite marked. However, it is important to recognize that these were fairly unique decades in terms of economic and labour market conditions, so making the contrast with the 1980s to the present appear especially marked. Irrespective of the precise term used to describe the effects of the changes in the labour market on young people's transition to adulthood, it is undeniable that their impact has been considerable. As Figure 4.2 illustrates, changes in the labour market have led to a vast increase in the possible permutations of routes from education to employment and to a lengthening of the process as a whole. In short, more young people are completing the transition (that is, via entering full-time employment) at a later chronological age than at any other time in modern British history. Data from the England and Wales Youth Cohort study, show that only just over half (54 per cent) of 18–19-year-olds were in full-time employment in 1991 (Park 1994).

Survey data on levels of unemployment, rates of participation in training schemes, full-time education, and the labour market show the extent of changes in the transition from education to employment since the 1960s. What do survey data reveal about changes in the second main component of the transition to adulthood, that of the family of origin to family of destination (or to some other form of independent household)? Data for the 1950s and 1960s show that these decades were marked by an acceleration of trends towards earlier ages at marriage, partly as a consequence of high rates of teenage marriage. Since then, there has been a *reversal* of the trend towards lower ages at family formation. Since the early 1970s, young people have begun to marry and/or have children at a later chronological age. Between 1971 and 1987, the average age at first marriage rose, from 21.4 years for women

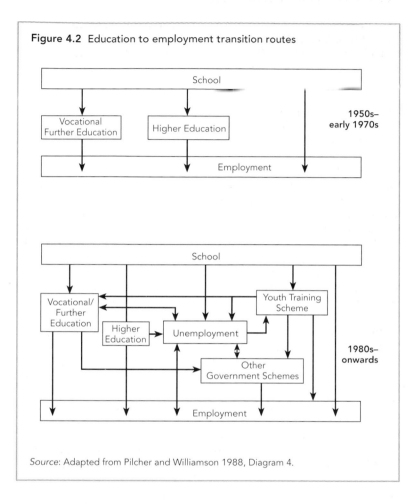

Figure 4.2 Education to employment transition routes

Source: Adapted from Pilcher and Williamson 1988, Diagram 4.

and 23.4 years for men, to 23.3 and 25.3 years respectively. Rates of teenage marriage have declined throughout the 1980s, from 1 in 4 marriages in 1980 to 1 in 18 in 1987 (Kiernan and Wicks 1990). Numbers of births per 1,000 women aged under 20 fell by 40 per cent between 1971 and 1986, and by 39 per cent for those aged 20–4 (Irwin 1990). Survey data also show that couples marrying since the late 1960s have been delaying starting their families. The average age at first birth for married women in 1970 was 24 years. By 1987, it had risen to 26.5 years (Kiernan and Wicks 1990).

At this point, it is important to recognize that the age at which young people experience key life course events, such as leaving the parental home, getting married, and having children (if they do at all) varies, especially by social class and by gender. Working-class young people and young women tend to experience these events at an earlier age than do middle-class young people and young men (Jones and Wallace 1992). Even so, the general trend since the end of the 1960s has been toward an increase in the chronological age at which these significant events in the life course are experienced.

In addition to higher ages at marriage and at first birth, there are other indications that the transition from family of origin to family of destination has changed over the last two decades. Kiernan and Wicks (1990) present data which show that, since the 1980s, there has been an increase in the proportion of families with older resident children. They suggest that this trend, along with those relating to age at marriage and at first birth, may be associated with changes in the economic structure which have impacted significantly on young people in their transition from education to employment. Hutton (1991) used survey data to compare the experiences of two cohorts of young people, one aged 16 in 1968 and the other aged 16 in 1978. The study compared the number of events, such as having left home, being in full-time work, and being married, which the young people had achieved by a given age. Hutton found that young people in the 1978 cohort had made slower progress in achieving these events than those in the 1968 cohort, and argued that this was a consequence of the 1978 cohort's greater exposure to unemployment.

Evidence on the timing of events such as marriage and having children indicates that significant changes have occurred since the early 1970s. On the surface, there would seem to be a link between changes in the transition to employment and changes in the transition to family of destination (or to some other form of independent household). The lengthening of the period of economic dependency of youth as a life course stage since the early 1970s would seem to have hindered young people's ability to secure the material resources necessary to support their transition from the parental home to a sexual partnership-based, independent home. However, caution must be exercised in explaining changes in the transition to family of destination *solely* in terms of changes in the transition from education to employment. The precise ways in which changes in the latter are related to changes in the former remain unclear. The indications are that courtship behaviour and patterns of marriage and childbirth have themselves undergone change since the 1970s. Thus, while survey data do show a rise in the average

age at marriage and a decline in the birth-rate to women in their 20s, data also show increased rates of cohabitation amongst young people and increased rates of birth outside marriage (Kiernan and Wicks 1990). Whilst in the immediate post-war decades there was a close link between the age at leaving the parental home and the age at marriage, there has been an emerging trend over the last two decades for young people to leave home and share flats or houses with their peer groups, before going to set up households with a sexual partner (Jones and Wallace 1992). As Hutson and Jenkins (1989) put it, changes in the household and family formation behaviour of young people 'bear the teeth marks' of changes in the economic structure and the labour market, but they are probably more strongly related to wider societal changes, including in the area of sexual morality, the impact of contraception and the influence of feminism. It was argued in Chapter Two that the life course, and the stages which comprise it, can be thought of as a social institution which is interconnected with other parts of the social structure. Youth as a stage of the life course in modern Britain is shaped by and embedded within the economic structure, family and household structures, the education system, and the social security system. All of these structures and institutions have undergone dramatic changes since the early 1970s; hence youth, as the transitional stage in the life course between childhood dependency and adult independence, has itself changed significantly. In particular, the *timing* and the *spacing* between the series of transitional events that comprise youth have changed, as well as the relationships between them. As Jones and Wallace (1992) explain, in the nineteenth and early twentieth century, there was a wide spacing between the various elements of the transition to adulthood. The middle part of the twentieth century, the 1950s and 1960s, saw a narrowing of the spacing, particularly between leaving home, marriage, and birth of first child. In the last few decades of the twentieth century, the spacing between such events is widening once more.

Changes in the labour market since the early 1970s have not prevented young people from becoming adults, even though the status of full-time worker is an important part of adult identity and the economic resources it brings are crucial in supporting the acquisition of adult roles and responsibilities. As Hutson and Jenkins (1989) explain, employment is only one aspect of adulthood. There are psychological and social pressures which lead young people into adulthood, their lack of economic independence notwithstanding. Yet, over the last two decades in Britain, the life course stage of youth has, for some young people at least, been formally extended. Jones and Wallace (1992) show

how state welfare policies have increasingly transferred responsibility for young people away from the state to their families. Social security benefits have become increasingly age-graded and, under housing benefit rules, young people are not 'adult' despite the legal age of majority being 18, until they are 26 years old. Such changes mean that young people without secure, full-time, and reasonably well-paid employment find it difficult to leave the parental home and maintain their own home. For these reasons, Jones and Wallace conclude that the 'transition to adulthood is now structured by access to employment to a greater extent than ever before' (1992: 103).

This chapter has mainly focused on historical comparisons of youth as a stage in the life course in modern Britain. Whilst it is apparent that changes have taken place within youth as a life course stage since the end of the 1960s, the 1950s and 1960s were themselves a marked change from previous decades. It is clear from this evidence that it is neither physiology nor chronology that determines the characteristics of youth as a social category or the experiences of young people within youth. Rather, youth is shaped by cultural, economic, and political practices. Experiences and opportunities within youth are shaped by specific cultural contexts, within historical time.

Whilst in some cultural traditions, as was illustrated earlier, the moment of transition to adulthood is quite definite, in modern Britain, changes in recent decades have made becoming an adult even more of an imprecise transition than it previously was. Earlier in this book, a case was made for the life course to be viewed as a cumulative, interconnected process. The way in which youth and adulthood are interconnected has no doubt been evident throughout the present chapter. The close links between these two stages of the life course will again feature, as the focus of attention now moves to adulthood itself.

Further Reading

Brake (1980, 1985) offers an analysis of youth culture. Female youth culture is the specific focus of McRobbie and Nava's (1984) *Gender and Generation*. A good starting-point for research on ethnic minority youth culture is Hewitt (1990). Jones and Wallace (1992) provide an up-to-date review of research on changes to youth transitions during the 1980s.

Chapter Five

Adulthood and Middle Age

Adulthood is the stage of the life course that children and young people are 'growing up' toward and that elderly people, in 'growing old', are moving away from. Judging by the ways in which children longingly anticipate it, as Chapter Three showed, adulthood would appear to be a status worth gaining. Concerns over the recent changes in young people's transition to adulthood, the focus of the previous chapter, also suggest the significance of adult status. As will be shown later in this chapter, and again in Chapter Six, those who are adult, but who are 'middle aged' or 'elderly', are concerned, in various ways, to retain their claims to adult status as they become 'old'. This evidence suggests that those who are not adults or whose adult status is under threat, accord great significance to adulthood: it is the central life course stage. The centrality of adulthood has less to do with its position mid-way through the span of human life than with its apparent *desirability*. Adulthood is a status that children and young people wait frustratedly for ('I can't *wait* until I'm grown-up!') and that old people struggle to retain ('I try to be independent'). This chapter explores the reasons why adulthood has 'ideological dominance' (Hockey and James 1993) as *the* stage in the life course in modern Britain. The role adult *bodies* play in sustaining the ideological dominance of the category 'adult' is considered. The issue of whether, in practice, all 'adults' enjoy adult status to the same extent is also examined. The remainder of the chapter focuses on middle age, a stage which marks the onset of threats to the 'youthfulness' of adult bodies and to the primacy of adult status more generally.

Adulthood has been described as an undifferentiated catch-all category about which we are insufficiently informed (Graubard 1978). Everyday conceptions are revealed when the commonly used term 'grown-up' is reviewed. It suggests that adult status is attained at a singular point and, further, that it is a once-and-for-all achievement, a plateau-like status with no significant pinnacles remaining. The term 'grown-up' therefore suggests that adulthood is a largely unproblematical status, once attained, forever retained. This taken-for-granted approach to adulthood is largely replicated in sociology's neglect of it as a stage in the life course. In the previous chapter, it became clear that assessing the precise impact of changes in the transition to employment and changes in family formation on young people's attainment of adult status is problematical, not least because of the vagueness and impreciseness of adulthood as a social category. In one sense, most sociology can be said to concern itself with the behaviour of adults; but this work largely takes age for granted (O'Donnell 1985). There are sociologies of childhood, of youth, and of old age, but there is no equivalent 'sociology of adulthood'. The neglect of adulthood as a social category may be a consequence of the tendency of many disciplines, sociology included, to focus on the growth and development phase of the human life span, namely childhood and youth. Adults are, by definition, socialized, developed, and 'grown'. Taking adulthood for granted has meant that little consideration has been given to it as a stage in the life course. The ways in which it is achieved, how adults differ from one another, how being an adult changes over historical time, individual time, and family time, and how adult behaviour is culturally conditioned, are all processes about which we remain 'insufficiently informed' (Graubard 1978).

Adulthood in History

Although knowledge about adulthood as a social category is limited, some research has been done on the ways in which adulthood emerged as a distinctive stage of the life course. When thinking about adulthood and its historical emergence, it is important to remember that the life course is best understood as an interconnected and cumulative process. The emergence of modern conceptions of childhood and of youth have already been discussed. The close links between their emergence, and that of old age, and the emergence of adulthood will become apparent in the following discussion.

The interrelations between conceptions of childhood, youth, adulthood, and old age are stressed by Hareven (1978) in her account of 'historical adulthood'. In pre-industrial Europe, as Aries (1962) has shown, children moved into adult life at a comparatively early age by modern standards. Gillis's (1974) work on the history of youth shows that in pre-industrial times, the meaning of youth did not correspond with modern conceptions, in that it referred to a semi-dependent worker-like status lasting from age 7 to the late twenties. At the other end of the life course, as detailed in Chapter Six, adults moved into old age and death without the moratorium stage of formal retirement from paid work, as is the practice in modern Britain. In short, participation in productive work roles, which, in modern societies are largely associated with adulthood, stretched over an entire lifetime. Children, young people, and the old all had productive work roles. This is undoubtedly linked to the fact that families operated as units of production as well as consumption, there being minimal separation of home and work. Hareven points out that participation in parenthood, the second of the two major adult roles in modern societies, also stretched over a large proportion of an individual's life span. Although people married and had children relatively late in life, their life expectancy was much shorter than it is in modern times. The combination of late age at family formation and short life expectancy, coupled with high rates of fertility, meant that it was rare for parents to experience an 'empty nest'. Once it had been entered into, parenthood to dependent children was, for all intents and purposes, a lifelong activity. Even under the apprenticeship system as described by Gillis (1974), this combination of factors meant it was highly unlikely that parents enjoyed a time without any dependent children living at home. In summary, then, in European pre-industrial society, 'demographic, social and cultural factors combined to produce only a minimal differentiation in the stages of life' (Hareven 1978: 205).

Previous chapters have considered the ways in which processes linked to industrialization impacted upon the nature of childhood and youth. In particular, children and young people became progressively excluded from the world of formal paid employment and enclosed within the education system. A similar process of *exclusion* affected older people, as retirement, at a specific chronological age and supported by an old age pension, became institutionalized by the early twentieth century (see Chapter Six). In this way, then, adulthood emerged through a process of exclusion, that is, of the exclusion of *prior* and *subsequent* stages of the life course. The demographic changes of the nineteenth century in turn impacted upon the nature of parenthood as a role which, formerly, had stretched over most of an individual's life. Trends toward lower fertility rates and increased longevity meant that parenthood to dependent children came to occupy a more compressed and specific period of the life course. In these ways, modern adulthood emerged as a stage, distinctive from prior, and subsequent, stages (Hareven 1978).

Jordan (1978) argues that a further factor influencing the emergence of adulthood was the gradual extension of the suffrage. Applying his argument to Britain, as working-class men and, finally, in 1928, all women, were given the right to vote, politically only adulthood mattered. The enfranchisement of the male working classes meant that class no longer excluded men from having the vote. The full enfranchisement of women later meant that gender no longer excluded individuals from having the vote. In terms of gaining this key political citizenship right, it was only *adult* status that mattered.

The above analysis indicates some of the ways in which adulthood came to be more clearly defined as a stage in the life course. The exclusion of children and old people from productive work roles and the eventual inclusion of adults, regardless of their class or sex, in a key right of political citizenship, can be recognized as factors which enhanced the desirability of adulthood as a prestige stage within the modern life course.

Hockey and James (1993) offer a broadly similar account of the emergence of adulthood as the dominant life course stage. Their analysis is concerned with exploring the attribution and withholding of 'personhood', a status symbolized through ideas of autonomy, self-determination, and choice, and of achieving full membership of a society. Hockey and James regard the exclusion of children and the elderly from the world of work as important developments contributing to their lesser personhood, but argue that the influence of individualistic values, and the values of the aspiring middle classes of the nineteenth century, upon these processes of exclusion must also be taken into account. Individualism in Britain encouraged a market-oriented approach to life and so brought with it a particular conception of personhood, epitomized in the 'self-made man' of the nineteenth century. The linking of personhood with productive work roles was also influenced by the desire for social status amongst the rising middle classes at this time. According to Hockey and James's analysis, this grouping gradually appropriated aristocratic family forms, with dependent wife and children. This in turn, permeated down to the lower classes, in consequence of middle-class philanthropic concerns. Children, young people, and the elderly emerged as dependent categories of persons (as did women), and so labour force participation became central to the attribution and withholding of personhood. 'To be socially respectable—to be a whole person—an adult male required a place within the work society' (Hockey and James 1993: 54). In these ways, then, Hockey and James suggest, adulthood developed its desirable profile, as the exclusive embodiment of concepts of personhood, independence, and autonomy (1993: 37).

Adulthood In Modern Britain

Accounts of the historical emergence of adulthood are suggestive of the ways in which adulthood came to be the central stage of the life course, of how it came to embody certain desirable qualities. A brief review of the phrases and terms commonly linked to 'adult' or 'grown-up' in contemporary Britain serves to tease out some of these desirable qualities. We speak of the 'responsible adult', implying that adults are sensible, reliable, and take or have responsibility for others. We speak also of 'a grown adult' or 'a grown woman' (or man). The implication here is that such a person is, therefore, able to decide upon a course of action in an autonomous and fully informed way. 'Grown adults' can go where they want, do what they want, but they also have to face up to and accept their responsibilities. Another phrase, 'mature adult', suggests that such a person is reasonable, calm, sensible, and able to solve problems using these qualities, without resorting to tantrums, sulking, or the use of violence. A final example is the phrase 'We are all grown-ups here', which suggests that individuals so present should not be reticent or coy, particularly about sexual matters or other such areas of exclusively 'adult' knowledge. Supportive evidence that adulthood is associated with particular qualities is provided by Hutson and Jenkins's (1989) study of young people and their parents. Notions of responsibility and independence were found to be core components of conceptions of adulthood.

It was shown in Chapter Four that official definitions of adulthood rarely coincide. Hutson and Jenkins (1989) suggest that official criteria do operate to define adulthood, albeit somewhat inconsistently. It is a status which is legally and administratively defined by the state and is recognized as a basic category of social membership (1989: 94). The above cited examples of phrases and terms commonly linked to 'adult' or 'grown-up' indicate that adulthood is also 'a set of practical accomplishments' and 'a repertoire of appropriate behaviour' (Hutson and Jenkins 1989: 95). For further evidence on the 'set of practical accomplishments' that mark adulthood, we can turn to data from the most recent sweep of the National Child Development Study (NCDS) (Ferri 1993). The cohort, first studied in 1958 when they were born, were last studied at age 33. The author of the report describes this age as being characterized by the settled and stable features of mature adulthood. Ferri found that, by the time they were 33 years old, 88 per cent of the men and 93 per cent of the women had had at least one 'live-in' relationship, including marriage. At the time of the study, 80 per cent were currently in a 'live-in' relationship. Around 67 per cent of the cohort had become parents by the age of 33. In terms of their participation in employment, 89 per cent of the men and 36 per cent of the women were working full-time (32 per cent of the women worked part-time). Almost 80 per cent of the sample were owner-occupiers, that is, they had bought or were paying a mortgage on their own home. On the basis of these data, then, adults in modern Britain tend to live with sexual partners, have children, work in paid employment, and maintain their own home.

At this point, it is important to remember that adulthood is a variable concept. The activities and behaviours exhibited by the 33-year-olds in the NCDS sample may be specific to this particular cohort of adults. Further, it has been suggested (Willis 1984) that whilst employment and a wage are important criteria of adulthood for men, motherhood is an important criterion of adulthood for women. However, Hutson and Jenkins (1989) found that amongst young people and their parents in South Wales, models of adulthood were undifferentiated by gender. A 23-year-old single mother was regarded as an adult by herself and her parents, but Hutson and Jenkins argued this had more to do with how she had responded to the responsibilities of having a baby than the fact of motherhood itself. It is unlikely, then, that male and female models of adulthood are as disparate as linking one with employment and the other with motherhood would suggest. Nevertheless, repertoires of behaviour in adulthood may be gendered in other ways, and may also vary by social class, ethnicity, and region of the country.

Wallace (in Jones and Wallace 1992) offers a way of organizing the various components of adulthood, including official markers, sets of practical accomplishments, and repertoires of behaviour. Wallace argues that, instead of the rituals which mark the attainment of adult status in some pre-industrial societies, modern Britain has 'markers' of status. These markers of status can be determined and ratified in three ways: privately, publicly, or officially. Private markers might include a first sexual encounter, or first cigarette. Public markers might include a wedding or other such event or occurrence which draws recognition from family and community. Official markers might include the right to vote or the granting of a bank loan. 'The important point is that adult status may have different meaning in the private, public and official spheres, but may require recognition in each sphere' (Jones and Wallace 1992: 102).

It can be concluded, then, that a range of criteria, markers, and signifiers serve to distinguish adult status. Hutson and Jenkins explain it in the following way: 'in addition to its existence as an officially defined identity—something which an individual *is*—adulthood is also understood as a set of practical accomplishments . . . something which an individual *does*' (1989: 05, original emphasis).

The ideological dominance of adulthood (Hockey and James 1993) arises from its association with concepts of independence and autonomy and with the citizenship rights and responsibilities that being an adult opens the door to. Hockey and James (1993) argue that the ideological dominance of adulthood, its exclusive profile as the embodiment of concepts of independence and autonomy, is sustained through practices or strategies which operate to *distance* other groupings from it and its desirable qualities. One such practice identified by Hockey and James is the 'infantilization' of old and disabled people, where they are treated *as if they were children*. This practice serves to 'conceptually distance' adults from physical or mental impairment; by transforming old and disabled adults into children, independence, attractiveness, and personhood are qualities secured solely for adulthood proper. Distancing others from the category 'adult' serves to define and delineate the limits of that category. Thus whatever adults are and whatever adults do, other categories, especially children and the elderly, are not and should not do.

In modern Britain, it is adults who dominate the social world. It is they, not children, young people, or the old, who hold positions of importance in families and households, in the labour force, in political institutions, and so on. It is adults who have control over material resources, both personal and institutional. In short, it is adults who make the world go around. Yet, not every adult has equal power and control and this is where thinking about adulthood in citizenship or personhood terms is useful. Partly as a consequence of the ways in which it is administratively defined by the state, adulthood is closely bound up with citizenship and personhood (Hutson and Jenkins 1989; Hockey and James 1993). Access to citizenship rights is now recognized to be structured by social class, gender, ethnicity, sexuality, and able-bodiedness, as well as age. This means that reaching the official age of adulthood, the legal age of citizenship or of 'majority', does not guarantee full or equal access to citizenship rights. Able-bodied, white, middle-class males in full-time employment are probably the most fully adult members of British society. Their advantageous structural position enables them to exercise their citizenship rights, their independence and autonomy, to a greater extent than can women, elderly or disabled people, children, the working class, or members of ethnic minority groups. Adulthood, when examined in terms of ideas of citizenship or personhood, begins to reveal itself as a rather more differentiated status than the orientational metaphor 'grown-up' suggests. Clearly, some grown-ups are more grown-up than others. Linguistic practices, such as referring to women as 'girls' and, in the American south, black men as 'boys' serve to confirm that adulthood is not a status enjoyed by all categories of adults to the same extent. For sure, adulthood is a rather complex status, and it is far from being a matter of simple physical or chronological maturity.

A developing theme within this book is the importance of interpretations placed upon physiological indicators of age, via the body. We have seen, for example, that children's bodies, in modern British culture, are 'read' in certain ways, a selective reading which informs perceptions of their vulnerability and dependency. In addition to the ways in which adults sustain their dominance through strategies such as infantilization of the elderly and the disabled, and the ideology of childishness which shapes adult–child relations, Hockey and James (1993) argue that adult *bodies* are important vehicles through which dominance is sustained. In popular culture, adults are encouraged to pay great attention to their bodies. They are exhorted to be physically fit, to eat and drink healthily, to control their weight, to take good care of their skin and hair with the aid of cosmetic products, and to wear fashionable and stylish clothes and footwear on their bodies. All these can be interpreted as manifestations of a concern to retain the qualities of adulthood. 'Having overcome the social and physical limitations of dependent childhood, the adult is portrayed as threatened with the subsequent loss of dominant status and power through the predations of the ageing process' (Hockey and James 1993: 81). Within popular culture, it is young, strong, toned, fit, and slim bodies which are portrayed as the most desirable bodies to have. Fit, well-groomed bodies act to bolster the adult individual's social power and status (Hockey and James 1993). The importance of a 'youthful' (that is, fit, healthy, toned, sexually attractive, and, to a certain degree, powerful) body, over which an individual has control, is evident in the next section, as the focus of attention turns toward adulthood in terms of 'middle age'.

Middle Age

Although sociological conceptions of adulthood remain largely undifferentiated, 'middle age' has been recognized as a relatively distinct stage within adulthood. In contemporary Western society, middle age is often thought to begin as young as age 35 (Brookes-Gunn and Kirsch 1984). Featherstone and Hepworth (1989) also note that ages 35–60 are increasingly considered as the 'mid-life' stage, whilst a recent Carnegie Inquiry defined middle age as the 'Third Age' of life (see box below), covering the years 50–74 (Sanders 1993). As always, assigning precise chronological markers to stages of the life course is extremely problematical. In the case of middle age, however, having a sense of current chronological markers is important, since research suggests that chronological definitions of middle age have undergone change in modern industrial societies, such as Britain. As we shall see, markers of middle age are argued to have shifted upwards over historical time, so that individuals are now thought of as middle aged at a later chronological age than previously.

THE THIRD AGE

The *First Age* is the period of childhood, characterized by socialization and dependent status.

The *Second Age* is the period of full-time employment, family building, and adult responsibility.

The *Third Age* covers the years 50–74 and is the age of active independent life, post-work and post-parenting.

The *Fourth Age* is old age proper, characterized by increasing dependence on others.

Sources: Bernard and Meade 1993b; Craig 1993.

Chronological age is rarely a precise marker of life course stages and middle age is no exception. Supplementary markers of middle age in contemporary Britain may include physical and social indicators. Thus, the onset of middle age may be indicated by a proliferation and intensification of the signs of ageing, including greying hair and the appearance of the 'middle aged spread'. For women, middle age status may be marked by the menopause, a physiological process which signals the end of a woman's reproductive capacities. Social indicators of middle age may include a change in parenting status (for those who have children), as the 'nest empties' of dependent children. The balance of activities between employment, family, and leisure may also change during the middle years of life, with less time taken up with family and work commitments and more time available for leisure pursuits. Emotionally, the middle years of life may be a time of intense reflection and contemplation, as suggested by the phrase 'mid-life crisis'. These various chronological, physical, and social markers of middle age are suggested here to provide a sense of the possible characteristics of this stage of the adult life course. The extent to which any or all of these markers have significance in practice in modern Britain will be a theme of the remainder of this chapter.

Featherstone and Hepworth, on the basis of their research on the cultural aspects of ageing, suggest that the middle years of life have undergone a process of reconstruction. Particularly since the end of the Second World War, they argue, the middle years of life have become redefined as 'mid-life'. This process of reconstruction is characterized by Featherstone and Hepworth as amounting to a 'new middle age'. Featherstone and Hepworth have written about the 'new middle age' in several publications and the following account draws on this literature to summarize the main points of their argument. According to Featherstone and Hepworth, the 'traditional' view regarded middle age as a natural and inevitable stage of life, characterized by normal and unavoidable signs of ageing, including wrinkles, grey hair, stiffness of limbs, and a bulging shape (Hepworth 1987). To this extent, the middle years of life were conceptualized as the end of youth and the beginning of old age. However, given the short life expectancies in past centuries, negative perceptions attached to physical signs of ageing were particularly significant. As Hepworth (1987) puts it, after middle age, most people could not realistically expect a long future. Long-term and gradual shifts in the image of middle age, away from the traditional view, are argued by Featherstone and Hepworth to be detectable from as early as the eighteenth century. Socially advantaged persons in British society at this time showed interest in matters of medicine and health and their potential value in prolonging youthful life (Featherstone and Hepworth 1990). Such a sensitivity to ageing, and interest in delaying it, continued throughout the nineteenth and early twentieth centuries. Interest was particularly heightened, though, in the 1920s and 1930s, as people 'flocked to the seaside, watched their diets, swallowed pills, sweated in Turkish baths and invented taxing physical activities, partly to ensure that they aged in a moral way' (Featherstone and Hepworth 1990: 269). Increasingly, then, the body was viewed as a sign of a person's moral character. Signs of ageing upon the body were regarded as a revealing guide to the moral life that a person had led. As a consequence, the ageing process was to be deferred and controlled for as long as possible. A 'youthful' appearance was the ideal, and 'premature' ageing something to avoid and battle against. So, as life expectancy has increased during the twentieth century the bodily indicators of ageing, which proliferate during middle age, have been challenged. For most people, there are now a lot of years left to live after their first appearance (Hepworth 1987). The reconstruction of middle age can be seen as an attempt to establish an ever-increasing distance between the middle years of life and old age and death.

Since the Second World War, middle age has increasingly been presented as a time for 'taking stock' and for 'self-development', as evident in an outcrop of popular books on middle age (Featherstone and Hepworth 1989). From the 1970s onwards, the concept of the 'mid-life crisis' has been taken more seriously and interpretations placed upon the female menopause have changed, along with the 'discovery' of the male menopause. Hepworth (1987) argues that over the last few decades, the public definition of the female menopause has altered. Once regarded as a 'silent crisis', the menopause is now celebrated as a prelude to personal and sexual liberation and portrayed as a fresh beginning. This new interpretation of the female menopause, Hepworth argues, has had significant repercussions for ideas about *male* middle age. In particular, the 'male menopause' is now recognized as a phenomenon marked by psychological and social transitions, if not physical ones. Hepworth concludes that the menopause has become a convenient metaphor for the expression and consciousness of 'the new middle age'.

Change in the meanings attached to the menopause is one indication that the middle years of life have undergone reconstruction. A second important trend identified by Featherstone and Hepworth is changes in the images of retirement. Their analysis is focused on a magazine aimed at near-retired and retired people, which first appeared in 1972. Entitled *Retirement Choice*, the magazine set out to dismantle traditional images of retirement, which associated retirement with a passive, largely inactive old age. The concern was to establish retirement as a 'positive' stage in life, characterized by liveliness and activity. During the 1970s, the magazine underwent several changes of title, something which in itself is indicative of changing images of retirement: from *Retirement Choice*, to *Pre-Retirement Choice*, to simply *Choice*. Throughout, the magazine presented retirement as an 'extended leisure lifestyle within which any infirmities that old age may bring can be managed with dignity and skill' (Featherstone and Hepworth 1990: 272). In these ways, the magazine *Choice* reflects the changing aspirations of recent cohorts of retirees who regard themselves as at a distance from the traditional image of middle age as the end of youth and the beginning of old age.

The 'new middle age' can be said, then, to intersect around the concept of 'youthfulness' and the capacity for personal and social change brought about by the transitions that are associated with the middle years of life. Featherstone and Hepworth summarize their argument in the following way. They write,

> during the last twenty to thirty years middle age has increasingly become a cause for concern. The public stereotype of middle age as a kind of 'mature' interlude with relatively unambiguous physical and psychological boundaries between young adulthood and declining old age, has been replaced by an ideal of active, prolonged mid-life which has more in common with youth than [old] age. (Featherstone and Hepworth 1989: 152)

Featherstone and Hepworth (1989) detect a strong cohort or social generational factor acting upon the process of reconstruction within middle age over the last few decades. They argue that the 'new middle age' is linked to the fact that the post-Second World War 'baby boomers' are now entering the middle age stage of life. It was this large cohort which engaged in the youth cultures of the 1950s and 1960s and enjoyed an advantageous position in the labour market. As this cohort enter middle age, they are bringing with them many of the values and cultural tastes of their youth, and are reconstructing what it means to be middle aged in the process.

The reconstruction of the middle age stage of the life course is further indicated by the popularization in recent years of the term 'the third age' and the development of organizations of so-called 'third agers'. One example here is the 'University of the Third Age', or 'U3A'. There are 212 Universities of the Third Age in Britain which offer around 200 distinct courses. The U3A does not offer degrees or qualifications, but operates as a 'self-help' community. Distinctions between tutors and students (or 'members') are blurred and the emphasis is on adults in the later stages of their lives, coming together to stimulate each other through teaching and learning (Craig 1993).

In their writing on the 'new middle age' Featherstone and Hepworth are careful to stress that there has not been a complete break from more traditional images of middle age. In particular, they acknowledge that *middle class* middle-aged individuals, with high levels of income and who have planned for their retirement, are more likely to be in a position to engage in an active, leisurely life-style, to enjoy high consumption of the goods and services which are increasingly marketed at the middle-aged, and to engage in 'body maintenance' (Featherstone and Hepworth 1989). The Carnegie Inquiry into the third age also recognized that, while this time of life can be marked by greater independence and freedom to engage in leisure pursuits, some people do not have the financial resources to support a third age life-style (Sanders 1993). The suggestion is, then, that although there are significant trends towards a 'new middle age', many individuals who are experiencing the transitions associated with the middle years of life remain relatively untouched by it. The rest of this chapter develops this important point further and examines evidence which indicates contrasting experiences of middle age for some groups within society.

Women are one of the social groups identified by the Carnegie Inquiry as having restricted access to a third age life-style. Due to their intermittent employment histories and tendency to work in low-paid jobs, women are at greater risk of poverty than men as they grow older (see Chapter Six). Consequently, women are less likely to secure the financial resources necessary to support participation in an active, leisure-based 'new middle age'. Women's patterns of participation in employment may also mean that middle age is a time when women *return* to the labour market having raised their children. Middle age, then, for women, may be marked by transitions into part-time employment, or from part-time employment to full-time employment (Main 1988), rather than withdrawal.

The question of how meaningful the 'new middle age' is for women is addressed by Bernard and Meade (1993*b*). They examine various constraints which restrict women's experience of leisure in later life. One important constraint is the tendency for women's work activities in the domestic sphere to intertwine and integrate with their leisure interests. Activities such as gardening, cooking, sewing and knitting, or participation in voluntary work may be viewed as both work *and* leisure. Bernard and Meade cite studies which, in any case, show that some groups of women feel that they do not deserve leisure time. Women are socialized into placing the needs of others before their own and so may feel guilt at indulging in leisure pursuits. Women may also be constrained from certain leisure activities due to disapproval shown towards women who, for example, go out on their own to pubs or go out without their partners. 'Concepts of socially acceptable and respectable activity, based on constructs of female sexuality, continue to hold considerable sway' (Bernard and Meade 1993*b*: 163).

Women are further restricted in their pursuit of leisure and pleasure within their middle age by their fear of male violence, a fear which may discourage them from travelling in the dark or being out on their own. Such fears may be greater for some ethnic minority women, who also have to contend with anxiety about racist violence. This restriction on women's mobility, Bernard and Meade note, is further exacerbated by the fact that women are less likely to hold a driving licence than men. This represents a severe constraint, given that a whole range of leisure and educational pursuits are facilitated by car ownership (1993*b*: 164). Bernard and Meade also point to the greater pressures women face about signs of ageing on their bodies. Middle-aged women struggle with sexism as well as ageism (see also Chapter Six), making it more difficult for them to participate in sport or other fitness activities as part of a 'body maintenance' programme. Finally, Bernard and Meade cite survey evidence which suggests that access to 'leisure time' is, in any case, gendered, so that whilst a retired man has 92 hours' free time a week, a retired woman has only 75 hours. Throughout the life course, women remain more occupied than men with family and domestic responsibilities, so reducing their 'free time'. Bernard and Meade's overall conclusion is that, in middle age, the impact of gender is not diluted (1993*b*: 166). From this evidence, it can be argued that women are likely to find it more difficult than men to achieve a 'new middle age' life-style.

There is a second grouping within the population of modern Britain who may also find the notion of a new middle age or third age life-style rather meaningless: those who are experiencing changes in the transition *from* employment. Sociologists have detected trends toward more ragged, less tidy exits from the labour force in the post-war decades. Schuller (1987), for example, argues that 'workending' is conventionally seen as a discrete event that takes place at a given point in time. This image of formal retirement, a rite of passage marked, perhaps, by a retirement party or a retirement gift, may be changing. Schuller describes an emerging *process* of workending, whereby individuals may experience a 'tapering down' of the intensity of employment over a period of years. This 'tapering down' may be initiated by being made redundant in the late forties or early fifties, then working at a casual or part-time job at a lower occupational level, followed by a period of unemployment. A second way in which workending may be changing, according to Schuller, is in the collective sense. Each individual within a given cohort may continue to make a conventional abrupt transition from employment to retirement, but the chronological age at which this takes place may become more and more diverse. Retirement would then lose its conventional clear-cut pattern of a cohort moving up to a specific chronological age at which all members then experience the transition at a single point. Schuller sees parallels here with changes in youth to adulthood transitions, which have become ambiguous and ill defined in nature (see also Chapter Four). The transitional period of middle age has undergone a similar process of change, particularly in terms of workending (Schuller 1987).

Laczko (1989) also points to recent trends in patterns of early exit from the labour force which mean that the transition from employment to retirement is becoming increasingly complex. The collapse of the labour market for older workers has meant that more are entering retirement involuntarily and after a period of long-term sickness or long-term unemployment, rather than directly from employment. Laczko argues that these changes in the transition from employment in middle age have negative implications for economic well-being and so for how individuals experience their middle age and period of retire-ment. Evidence about changes in 'workending' can be used to qualify arguments about the emergence of a 'new middle age' or 'third age' life-style. Falls in economic activity amongst older workers in the years immediately preceding formal retirement age (see Table 5.1), may mean that those who are experiencing early or ragged exits from the labour force have not built up sufficient financial resources to support a 'leisure and pleasure' focused life-style in their middle age. In partic-ular this may be the experience of those in unskilled and semi-skilled manual employment, who are likely to be vulnerable to periods of unemployment and redundancy in their late forties and fifties and who are more likely to rely solely on a state rather than an occupational pen-sion scheme (Laczko 1989). Since, generally speaking, black and Asian members of the ethnic minority communities are over-represented in less skilled manual occupations and are more prone to unemployment (Abercrombie *et al.* 1994), these groupings may be disproportionately disadvantaged in their access to the new middle age.

Table 5.1 Economic activity of men, 1975–1992 (%)

Age	1975	1985	1992
45–54	98	93	90
55–9	94	82	78
60–4	84	53	52
65+	16	8	7

Source: OPCS 1994b.

In assessing trends toward a 'new middle age' or 'third age', there is a range of evidence to consider. On the one hand, there is evidence, such as that discussed by Featherstone and Hepworth, of an emerging trend whereby people in middle age are concerned to extend their middle age, and distance themselves from old age, by cultivating a positive, active 'youthful' life-style. In recent decades, there have emerged specialist publications aimed at the middle-aged, including regionally such as *The Mature Tymes* in South Wales, a 'news magazine for the over 50s'. There have been a series of programmes broadcast on daytime television such as 'Prime Time' and 'Whatever Next', also aimed at the middle-aged. New patterns of consumption by the middle-aged are further indicated by the way in which, for example, holiday companies and insurance companies market their products at the 'fiftysome-things' and upwards. Such developments do seem to indicate that what it is to be middle-aged is becoming redefined and its chronological markers extended upwards, past the formal retirement ages.

On the other hand, evidence reviewed by Bernard and Meade (1993b) and trends documented by Schuller (1987) and Laczko (1989) point to there being a 'disparity of prospects' (Sanders 1993) within middle age. Women and those who experience ragged or early exits from full-time employment may find their circumstances in middle age are not conducive to participating in a 'leisure and pleasure' based life-style. The extent to which individuals can enjoy a 'new middle age' is heavily dependent upon access to financial and other resources, including time and health, and this in turn is influenced by the extent to which individuals have been able to accumulate these resources at earlier stages of their life course. Whilst the 'new middle age' may contain a cohort or social generational component, as the post-war 'baby boomers' enter middle age and change the age norms associated with it, this factor is clearly cut across by gender, by class, and by ethnicity.

The debate about the 'new middle age' and its applicability to groups other than white, middle-class males, again serves to underline the importance of recognizing that people are never just youths or middle-aged, but are also 'classed', 'raced', and 'gendered'. These positions within a system of structured inequality operate to differentiate experiences within middle age and within adulthood more generally. This chapter, in discussing the adult stage of the life course, has shown that it is a rather more fragmented status than the everyday concept of 'grown-up' suggests. Consequently, although adulthood can be said to have 'ideological dominance' (Hockey and James 1993) and adults identified as the dominant age group within society, some adults are clearly more 'grown-up' than others. The theme that status within the

life course is differentiated by, for example, gender, is further emphasized in the next chapter, where the focus of attention turns to the last
stage of the life course: old age.

Further Reading

Kerckhoff (1990) uses data from the fourth sweep of the NCDS, when
the cohort were aged 23 years old, and undertakes comparisons with
transitions to adulthood in America. Laslett (1989) writes about the
emergence of the third age, whilst Germaine Greer (1991) discusses
women, ageing, and the menopause.

Chapter Six

Later Life and Old Age

The title of this chapter is intended to signal the need for an aware-ness that, within the later stages of the life course, experiences are likely to be rather more varied than grouping everyone together in 'old age' might suggest. As Hockey and James (1993: 87) note, the social category 'the elderly' or 'old age pensioner' encompasses a huge age range, from 60 to 100 plus years old. It is necessary to acknowledge then, that dis-tinctions might need to be drawn within the stage of life commonly glossed over as 'old age'. This important point notwithstanding, the identification of 'old age' as the *final* stage of the life course is unavoid-able, given the finite span of human life. Every individual has an age and, from the moment of birth, grows older. Those individuals within the final stage of the life course, though, are *aged* and *have* grown old. In relative chronological terms at least, people in the last stage of the life course are 'elderly'. For them, it is certain that there are fewer of their birthdays ahead than have already been. Their death is a rather more likely event than previously. Whether this position in the last stage of the life course and the accumulation of a large number of chronological years means that people *feel* old or see themselves as old is one of the issues examined in this chapter. As in previous chapters, historical and cross-cultural evi-dence is reviewed to draw out the particular features of old age in mod-ern Britain. The main focus is on the social status and material position of older people. Here, particular attention is paid to the experiences of women, since, as is explained below, women make up a significant pro-portion of those within the last stage of the life course.

Old Age in Modern Britain

In comparison with the inconsistency with which young people are deemed officially 'adult', old age uniformly and officially begins at the age of retirement and eligibility for a state pension. Currently in Britain, this is at age 60 for women and 65 for men. Sociologists who write about old age also tend to use this chronological marker, largely because it is a rather convenient one. By age 65, over 90 per cent of people in Britain are no longer in paid work and are in receipt of a state pension (Arber and Ginn 1991). Other 'vital statistics' about older people in modern Britain can be found in the box below. Most sociologists, though, acknowledge the problematical nature of 60/65 years and over as a definition of who is 'old'. The chronological age span referred to as 'old age' can, in modern Britain, cover as many as forty years. Grouping all those aged 60/65 and above in one category tends to discourage an awareness of the range of experiences within 'old age'. Partly as a response to this, it has increasingly become conventional to draw distinctions between different stages of old age. However, as with old age itself, subdivisions tend to be drawn on the basis of chronological age. Those aged 65–74 are classified as the 'young elderly' or the 'young old', while those aged between 75 and 84 are the 'old elderly' or the 'old old'. A third category are the 'very elderly' or the 'oldest old', who are aged 85 and over. Such subdivisions within old age were originally made on the basis of likely health differences between old people of different ages.

STATISTICS ON PERSONS AGED 60 AND OVER IN MODERN BRITAIN, 1991

- *Marital Status*   %
  Married   57.3
  Widowed   30.6
  Single (never married)   8.2
  Divorced   3.7

- 38.3% of people aged 60 or over said they had a limiting long-term illness (a health problem or handicap which limited their daily activities)

- 63% of households did not contain any persons aged 60 or above
  37% of households contained one or more person aged 60 or above

- 38% of persons aged 65 and over lived alone
  39% lived with their elderly spouse
  6% lived with their son or daughter

- 47% of persons aged 65 and over had access to a car, but men were more likely to have access than women (59% compared to 38%)

- Less than 1% of persons aged 60–74 were in care, compared to over 5% of those aged 75–84 and 21% of those aged 85 and over

Source: OPCS 1993b; 1993c; 1994c.

However, as Arber and Ginn (1991) note, the divisions tend now to be routinely made on the basis of chronological age alone.

Numerically speaking, old age (using age 60/65 and above as a marker) has become an increasingly significant stage of the life course in twentieth-century Britain. There are now more old people, relatively and absolutely, than ever before. In 1901, under 5 per cent of the total population were aged 65 and over. By 1991, the proportion had risen to 16 per cent (Kiernan and Wicks 1990; Central Statistical Office 1994a). As Chapter One explained, this 'ageing of the population' is primarily due to lower fertility rates during the twentieth century, so that young people now make up a smaller proportion of the population than they did in the past. Nevertheless, the number of old people has increased significantly in aggregate terms. In 1901, there were just 1.7 million people aged 65 and over (Kiernan and Wicks 1990). By 1991, there were 10 million people over retirement age (60 for women, 65 for men) (Central Statistical Office 1994a). People are also living for longer within old age. During the second half of the twentieth century alone, the proportion of the population aged 80 and over increased from 1.9 per cent in 1961 to 3.7 per cent in 1991 (Central Statistical Office 1994a).

The Carnegie Inquiry into the third age describes as one of the great social achievements of the twentieth century the fact that, for the first time in history, most people can expect to live for twenty or thirty years after they have retired from full-time employment (Sanders 1993). Yet, judging by the 'new middle age', a reconstruction of middle age characterized by a concern to establish an ever-increasing distance between it and old age (see Chapter Five), old age is not a stage of life which is eagerly anticipated. A survey commissioned by Age Concern in 1992 revealed that four out of five young adults in Britain feared old age, with two-thirds citing either loss of independence or poor health as a predominant concern (cited in Hockey and James 1993).

Evidence that old age is a stage in the life course in modern Britain which is largely negatively perceived can be found in everyday descriptions of elderly people as being 'past it' and 'over the hill' or as having 'one foot in the grave' (Hockey and James 1993: 16). Old people may be referred to in derogatory or condescending ways, as in 'old fogey', 'old biddy', 'old bat', or 'sweet little old lady/man'. Common stereotypes of old age tend to be largely negative, as the survey by Age Concern demonstrated. Other evidence also shows that old age is commonly perceived to be a stage of life characterized by loneliness, ill health, and poverty. To stereotype old people in this way is, however, *ageist*, because of the assumption that their experiences within life are determined merely by their chronological age. Ageist stereotypes operate to 'create the notion that people cease to be people, cease to be the same people or become people of a distinct and inferior kind by virtue of having lived a specified number of years' (Comfort 1977, quoted in Thompson *et al.* 1991). As with all stereotypes, ageist stereotypes act to marginalize old people and differentiate them from people who are not deemed to be old. *Ageism* is the term which describes the prejudice and discrimination experienced by old people. As Figure 6.1 shows, it is a practice that Age Concern campaigns against.

Figure 6.1 Campaigning against ageism

Source: Age Concern. Reproduced with permission.

Ageism extends beyond mere name-calling or stereotyping by individuals. Arber and Ginn (1991) argue that ageism is reinforced and perpetuated within British culture and institutions. They point to the ways in which ageism is institutionalized in the labour market, for example. Older people face age barriers in employment and are compulsorily retired at a specific chronological age. Furthermore, eligibility for pensions and for concessionary leisure and travel facilities is also fixed at specific ages. Upper age limits exist for membership of statutory bodies and voluntary organizations. For example, older people are stopped from being active in the Girl Guide Movement from age 65, from holding office in the Women's Royal Voluntary Service at 65, and from being a member of a Community Health Council at age 70 (Midwinter 1990, cited in Bernard and Meade 1993*b*). Ageism also permeates the medical treatment of old people, from suggestions that they should not expect to feel fit and healthy because of their age, to excluding them from certain forms of treatment (Arber and Ginn 1991).

From the available evidence, old age would appear to be a stigmatized social identity. Even those who are chronologically old may disassociate themselves from 'old age'. Thompson and colleagues interviewed a sample of people who were aged 60 to 87 years old and found that 'whatever their chronological age, whatever their appearance, whatever their health and physical ability, and whatever their awareness of all these aspects of themselves, they almost unanimously did not think of themselves as old' (1991: 108). Thompson and colleagues concluded that dissociation from old age by 'old people' is understandable, in the light of the stereotypes and negativity attached to old age. The people interviewed by Thompson and colleagues defined old age mainly in terms of health and physical ability. If someone was incapacitated through ill health, then they were 'old'. However, some of those interviewed reported a degree of incapacitation and ill health and still did not 'feel old' in themselves. One 80-year-old woman said, 'Not really, I don't feel my age. It's just my legs that feel old, not me head. I don't feel nearly eighty' (quoted in Thompson *et al.* 1991: 112).

The link between the appearance of an older person's body and his or her stigmatized social identity is a strong one. For example, Hockey and James (1993) point to the way in which the adjective 'wrinkly' is used as a noun to refer to old people. They argue that this usage establishes a metonymical (or part-to-whole) relationship between the appearance of the body and the social identity of the person: 'through a highly selective reading of the body—its wrinkled skin—a single part of the person is substituted for the whole' (1993: 94). Yet, for the (chronologically) old people studied by Thompson *et al.* (1991), the appearance and functional ability of their own aged bodies, although recognized, did not operate to determine their own subjective age identities. They accepted that their hair was grey, their skin was wrinkled, and their bodies had 'slowed down', but they still did not feel old or think of themselves as old. It can be argued, therefore, that a tension or distance exists between, on the one hand, interpretations placed upon the external appearance and functioning of an old person's body by (younger) others, and on the other, the subjective sense of identity held by older people themselves. To this extent, signs of old age can be understood as a mask or disguise (Featherstone and Hepworth 1989: 151), which acts both to influence younger people's attitudes and behaviour toward old people and conceal the individuality of old people themselves.

In addition to the disparity between interpretations placed by others on elderly people's bodies and the significance attached to their bodies by old people themselves, there is also evidence that the experience of old age is often not as negative as it is stereotypically assumed to be. Hendricks and Hendricks (1979) cite American survey evidence which indicates that people under 65 years old consistently overestimated the severity of problems experienced within old age. For example, whilst 62 per cent of those under 65 expected the elderly to have insufficient income, only 15 per cent of the elderly themselves reported this as a very serious problem. Poor health was identified by 50 per cent and loneliness by 60 per cent of those aged under 65 as serious problems experienced by the elderly. Yet only 21 per cent and 12 per cent of elderly people respectively reported these as serious problems. British evidence is provided by Thompson *et al.* (1991). The old people in this study are described as being 'pleasantly surprised' that the reality of their lives was different from the negative stereotypical depictions of old age. The likelihood that people's experiences of old age often does not conform to the stereotype of it may be a further reason why 'old' is an identity from which many disassociate themselves.

Having established that old age tends to be negatively perceived in modern Britain, and that old people themselves are marginalized and subject to prejudice and discrimination, brief consideration can now be given to theories which attempt to explain why this occurs.

Disengagement theory falls within the functionalist perspective because of its emphasis on the functions of old people's marginalized position and stigmatized status. Associated with Cumming and Henry (1961), disengagement theory proposes that the gradual and progressive withdrawal of old people from work roles and social relationships is both an inevitable and natural process. It prepares society, the individual old person, and those with whom she or he has personal relationships for the ultimate disengagement: their death. Disengagement is a two-way process. Society withdraws from interaction with old people and old people themselves withdraw from society. Disengagement benefits old people themselves, as they become increasingly self-absorbed in preparation for their death. It is also a process which benefits society, since it means that the death of individual societal members does not prevent the overall and ongoing functioning of the social system. Various criticisms have been levelled against disengagement theory. Here, reference is made to criticisms raised by Bond, Briggs, and Coleman (1990: 30). First, in suggesting that disengagement is desirable, the theory tolerates, if not condones, indifference towards elderly people and their problems. Second, Bond, Briggs, and Coleman argue that disengagement is not a feature of old age *per se.* They point out that some people, regardless of age, never engage in intense levels of social interaction. Third, disengagement theory is criticized for underplaying the role cultural values and economic structures have in *creating* the disengagement of old people.

The Marxist influenced *political economy perspective* regards the economic and political structure, particularly of capitalistic societies, as of central importance in creating the position and status of old people. This perspective is associated with Townsend (1986) and Phillipson (1982), amongst others. The main argument of the political economy perspective on old age centres around the concept of structured dependency, whereby the dependent status of old people is the result of their restricted access to societal resources, especially income from employment. Data from the 1991 Census show that most old people live in households where no one is in employment. Of people aged 60 and above, only 28 per cent lived in households where someone was working. The figure decreases further amongst older people, so that only 18 per cent of those aged 65 and above, and 13 per cent of those aged 75 and above lived in households where someone was working (OPCS 1993*c*). From the political economy perspective, then, society is seen to create the problems of old age through economic, political, and cultural practices, such as the institution of retirement and the old age pension, and the operation of health and welfare services. These forms of institutionalized ageism are argued to have been developed to benefit the management of industry and the economy (Townsend 1986). Johnson is critical of the political economy perspective, arguing that a concentration on the concept of structured dependency has deflected attention away from more progressive and optimistic views of the economic and social status of old people in modern Britain (1989: 62). Johnson suggests that the economic position of old people has improved in the twentieth century, especially in relation to the security of their income from state benefits. However, in criticism of Johnson, evidence shows that there is a high incidence of poverty and low incomes amongst elderly people (Walker 1990). In 1991/2, 54 per cent of pensioner couples and 63 per cent of single pensioners had below average incomes (Department of Social Security 1994). The absolute economic position of the elderly may have improved during the twentieth century but old people continue to make up a large proportion of the poor in modern Britain. Social security benefits represent the largest source of income for elderly people (Table 6.1) and so the level at which these are set has an important influence on their living standards. In 1993, when the average weekly gross income for all households was £353, that for one-adult households dependent on state

Later Life and Old Age

Table 6.1 Income and sources of income amongst the elderly, 1993

	Gross weekly household income (£)	% of income from social security[a]	% of income from annuities and pensions[b]	Other sources[c]
All households	353	13.9	6.2	80
Head of household				
aged 65–75	216	42.7	26.3	30.2
aged 75+	152	54.4	24.5	21.1
retired	181	48.4	26.5	25.1

[a] Including the state retirement or old age pension
[b] Including employers' pension and private pension
[c] Including from wages and salaries, income from investments

Source: Central Statistical Office 1994b.

pensions was £73 (one fifth of the average) (Central Statistical Office 1994b).

Turner (1989) uses *exchange theory* to explain the stigmatization of old people in modern British society. He is critical of political economy perspectives, arguing that the status of old people cannot be explained simply by making reference to the economic and political needs of capitalism. Turner proposes that the stigmatization of old people results from their dependency within a society whose fundamental framework is one of social exchange and reciprocity. Old people are stigmatized because of their declining reciprocity as they grow older. Bernard and Meade (1993a) are critical of exchange theory in general, arguing that versions of it have helped fuel the pernicious debate about interage group conflict over scarce societal resources (see Chapter Seven).

Hockey and James (1993), like Turner, suggest that the status of personhood waxes and wanes over the life course in modern Britain. They argue (after Kohli 1988) that this process should be understood in the context of Britain as a 'work society'. In other words, in Britain, work operates as an important means of economic livelihood, as a key route to participation in consumer society and as a source of social and personal identity. Access to and participation in work consequently has great importance as an index of social worth, 'conceptually tying' high social status to participation in the labour market. 'Elderly people, like children, are accorded low social status through their marginal involvement in the work society . . .' (1993: 148), and so find themselves stigmatized in their dependency. Hockey and James's account of the ways

105

in which labour force participation came to be central to the attribution and withholding of personhood was outlined in the previous chapter.

Dowd employs a *cohort* or *social generational approach* in his explanation of the marginalized and stigmatized status of old people in modern Western societies. Older people's position in the historical social structure means that, in the present, they are considered as 'immigrants in time' and as 'strangers in their own land' (1986: 154). Old people appear strange in their aged physical features, and in their styles of clothing and preferences in entertainment, which seem old fashioned by contemporary standards. The values they hold and standards of behaviour they adhere to also seem strange. Dowd argues that old people's access to previous cultural and political events gives them a 'past-situated social identity', at least in the minds of those younger than themselves. At the basis of the cultural separation and social distance between older and younger people in society, Dowd argues, is a contrast in social generational world views, arising out of their differing locations in historical time. In pointing to the role cohort or social generational processes may play in the marginalization and stigmatization of older people, Dowd makes a valuable contribution to understanding older people's status in modern societies. However, his account can be criticized for stressing the *differences* that undoubtedly do exist between the cultures of older and younger people at the expense of the culture that they *share*.

All the theories considered so far can be said to be examples of the way in which theory both reflects and, albeit often inadvertently, contributes to, the general mood of pessimism about the role and status of older people (Fennell, Phillipson, and Evers 1988). A rare example of a theory which offers a more positive view on old age is *activity theory*. It is like disengagement theory, in that it falls within the functionalist perspective, via its emphasis on roles, and in its concern with the *adaptation* of people to old age. Activity theory, though, is also a counterpoint to disengagement theory, since it argues that a successful old age can be achieved by *maintaining* roles and relationships. Any loss of roles, activities, or relationships within old age should be replaced by new ones to ensure happiness and well-being. Activity theory has been criticized by Bond, Briggs, and Coleman (1990) for being unrealistic (after all, biological ageing does impose some limitations) and for underplaying economic, political, and social structural factors which place constraints on activity in old age. However, activity theory does seem to 'speak to' aspects of some older people's experiences. For the (chronologically) old people in Thompson's study, as we have seen, being old was not as bad as they had feared. Thompson (1992) shows how, for these old people, later life was a time of active challenges which required the use of various strategies in order to find meaning and fulfilment. These strategies included rebuilding intimate adult relationships and continuing in work roles.

Activity theory has been mentioned here mainly to slightly lighten the rather gloomy emphasis of this section. However, before going on to consider the status and position of old people in the past (and also in other cultures), an assessment of likely *future* trends with regard to the social status of the old in Britain is needed. Unfortunately, the indications are rather gloomy. Negative stereotypes of old age and prejudicial attitudes toward old people may increase in the light of the further ageing of the population. As is discussed in Chapter Seven, the projected rise in numbers of old people is increasingly viewed as a pressing social problem, particularly in terms of their consumption of state pensions and health and welfare services. As Arber and Ginn (1991: 50) note, the ageing of the population has made ageism more visible and more politicized, as concerns are raised about the distribution of scarce societal resources between the old and other age groups.

Old Age in History

This section looks at what is revealed by historical evidence on the status and position of old people. It is important to note at the outset that knowledge in this area is lacking, a fact which may have contributed to the common belief that in 'the good old days', old people were not as socially and economically marginalized as they are today.

As has been noted previously, family life and work life were more integrated in the pre-industrial past. This meant that old people were less likely to have experienced economic and social segregation. Moreover, a number of factors, including low life expectancy, meant that work and family roles were retained for most of an individual's life course. Differentiation between various life course stages, as we have seen in discussions of childhood, youth, and adulthood, was minimal. Certainly, in pre-industrial society, there was no formal retirement period supported by a state pension, for which individuals became eligible at a certain chronological age. Work stopped completely only with severe illness or death, although the nature of work engaged in by people is likely to have changed as they became older. The later years of life were probably marked by a move to less arduous work (Hareven 1978).

In pre-industrial Europe, 'old age' was not tied to any specific chronological age. Rather, definitions were loose and very varied (Roebuck 1978), attached to any of the decades after 40 or 50 depending upon the context (Pelling and Smith 1991). According to Featherstone and Hepworth, 'Old people were those who, regardless of chronological age, had become helpless and dependent and thus appropriate objects of charity' (1990: 263). Arriving at a specific chronological age created no entitlement to charity, poor relief, poor law pensions, or medical treatment, but was sometimes used to exempt older people from, for example, military service (Pelling and Smith 1991).

Evidence on social attitudes to old people in pre-industrial society is rather mixed. There are some indications that old people were accorded respect for their traditional knowledge, skills, and wisdom. Thompson and colleagues (1991) discuss evidence which suggests that the prevailing ideal was 'gerontocratic': communities were typically run by the 'ancientry of the parish' and important public figures, such as in the church and judiciary, were old men. However, other evidence points to rather more ambivalent attitudes toward the old in the premodern past. Images of old age, such as depicted in art (Featherstone and Hepworth 1990) or as in Shakespeare's description of it as 'second childishness' (see Box 2.1) do not portray it as a desirable stage of life. Historians now argue that contrasting stereotypes of old age in the past, some positive and some negative, reflect the fact that old people were not viewed or treated in a homogeneous way. In particular, material resources are argued to have been important in influencing attitudes toward old people. Featherstone and Hepworth (1990) argue that old age could never in itself command respect, and that those who had made little provision for an independent old age could find themselves despised and neglected. They quote one historian, who writes that 'The old man sitting at the fireplace was disregarded but if he "hath estate of his own to maintain himself and to pleasure his children, oh, then . . . his age is honoured, his person is reverenced, his counsel sought and his voice obeyed"' (Thompson 1976, quoted in Featherstone and Hepworth 1990: 262). In summary, then, historical evidence tends not to support the nostalgic belief that the past was a 'golden age' for old people, who, in part due to their scarcity, were venerated for their skills and wisdom. In theory, old people may have enjoyed a respected status and retained power and control over younger people. In practice, the evidence suggests that for old people with diminished physical, social, and material resources, prospects were bleak (Featherstone and Hepworth 1990).

The idea that the past was a 'golden age' for old people is associated with *modernization theory* (Cowgill and Holmes 1972). In this theory, the loss of status of old people is argued to be a product of industrializing society. New ideas and new technology, urbanization, greater geographical mobility, and enhanced longevity all combine to undermine the traditional respected status of old people (Pelling and Smith 1991). Modernization theory has become subject to increasing criticism, especially in the light of evidence, reviewed above, that not all old people enjoyed a venerated status in the past. Foner (1984) argues that the modernization model 'distorts and simplifies changes in age relations' and claims that changes in the status of old people are more complex and varied than it tends to suggest.

Although the precise impact of industrialization and associated changes on the position of old people continues to be debated, there are several key developments in the emergence of old age as a distinct stage in the modern British life course that can be highlighted. First, the development and introduction of old age pensions. Serious discussion of a state old age pension scheme began in the late nineteenth century (Roebuck 1978) and was legislated for in the 1908 Old Age Pension Act. The Act offered a pension for the 'very old, the very poor and the very respectable' (Thane 1978) and was available to persons at age 70. The second important development occurred in the decades after the First World War, when, in the context of unemployment and economic depression, the idea of retirement as an appropriate stage in the life course for elderly workers gained credence (Featherstone and Hepworth 1990). By the 1940s, retirement had been written into state support for the elderly and became part of a new institutionalized dependency (Macnicol and Blaikie 1989: 37). By the late 1960s, it was accepted that the normal period of full-time employment would cease for most of the population at age 60 for women and 65 for men (Harper and Thane 1989). The institutionalization of retirement can be recognized as one of the key factors in the social construction of old age as a distinct stage in the modern life course. In 1890–1 in Britain, around two-thirds of men over age 65 were economically active. By 1951, the proportion had fallen to one-third (Arber and Ginn 1991). In 1992, only 7 per cent of men aged over 65 were economically active (OPCS 1994*b*). The economic activity rates of women aged 65 and over have, historically, been lower than that of men and in the late 1980s only 3 per cent of women aged over 65 were in paid employment (Arber and Ginn 1991).

This review of evidence on the emergence of old age as a distinct life course stage has shown that nostalgia about the past being a golden age for old people is misplaced. At best, attitudes to those regarded as old were ambivalent. Old age as a distinct life course stage has a fairly recent origin. First, in the proportion of people who are in old age (defined by the retirement age). As we have seen, this has increased markedly during the twentieth century. Second, in the institutionalization of state pensions for the old from 1908 onwards. Third, in the institutionalization of retirement, the normality of which became more entrenched as the twentieth century progressed. In some ways, these developments can be said to have led to the improvement of the position and status of elderly people as Johnson (1989) suggests. In other ways though, these same developments can be argued to have contributed to the 'structured dependency' of elderly people in modern Britain.

Old Age in Cross-Cultural Perspective

Kagan (1980) studied old age in a Colombian peasant village in the Andes. She found that old age was not considered as an idle period of life. Individuals spent more time with their children and grandchildren and remained active, if physically capable, in wage earning and household tasks throughout their old age. Old people, then, retained a high level of integration in family and community activities. They did not constitute a gerontocracy with exceptional rights and privileges, but were esteemed and respected within the village. 'Deference for the aged is demonstrated in a quiet but sincere manner with respectful allowance being made for the childlike behaviour of the senile' (Kagan 1980: 67). Kagan's study provides evidence on the position and status of elderly people within one cultural tradition. The review of historical evidence of the elderly in Europe's pre-industrial past showed that old people were not treated in a uniform way. This variation in the status and position of the old is also indicated by cross-cultural evidence.

Every known society has been found to define persons as 'old', whether on the basis of chronology, physiology, or generation, but the position and status of the old within any one society is dependent upon the interrelationships of a variety of factors (Victor 1987). First, the type of social organization. For example, for nomadic peoples, frail and dependent old people represent a particular burden. Evidence suggests that in such societies, the old may be neglected, abandoned, or even ceremonially put to death. If the way of life is settled and family and work life are integrated, however, old people can continue to make a valuable contribution to economic, family, and cultural activities. A second set of factors relate to the extent to which the skills, experience, and knowledge of old people is exclusive to them and retains value for the society. For example, in Williams's (1980) study of American Indian elderly, he argues that elderly males are placed in a highly valued position for their previous roles of leadership and possession of tribal knowledge. A third set of factors relates to the extent to which old people exercise direct control over economic resources. If it is *through* old people that younger people gain access to economic resources, then their care and respect is more assured. A fourth set of factors relates to cultural attitudes toward death and the afterlife. For the Sherbro people of Sierra Leone, incoherent or incomprehensible speech by an aged person is perceived as a *positive* sign. Their incoherence indicates their close communication with ancestors, who are regarded as important arbiters of destiny (MacCormack 1985, cited in Hockey and James 1993). 'Within this context old people are cared for reverently as they grow into sacredness' (Hockey and James 1993: 96). As noted in the opening chapter, for the Venda-speaking people of southern Africa, old age is regarded as a 'pleasure'. Signs of old age, such as greying hair or the birth of a grandchild, are welcomed as indications of a person's approaching contact with the 'real' world of the spirits (Hockey and James 1993: 92). In cultures where the afterlife is accorded great significance, old people's proximity to death enhances rather than reduces their status.

Cross-cultural evidence shows that there are a variety of understandings of old age and experiences within it. Signs of old age are not universally stigmatized, nor are old people uniformly excluded from productive work roles. If they do withdraw from work activities, their dependency on their children is not always perceived in negative terms. In short, both historical and cross-cultural evidence shows that the position and status of old people in modern Britain is culturally and historically specific and should be recognized as such.

Women in Old Age

Historical and cross-cultural evidence shows that old people have not tended to be treated in a uniform way. In contemporary Britain, recognition that old people are not a homogeneous group has increased. Research evidence shows that access to financial and material resources, health resources, and domestic/caring resources (Arber and

Ginn 1991) varies by gender, social class, and ethnicity. The remainder of this chapter focuses on the experiences of women in old age. In the words of Bernard and Meade (1993*a*), old age is very much an issue for, and about, women.

The structure of the British population varies by gender, with the ratio of women to men becoming particularly skewed in the latter stages of the life course. In 1992, the ratio of females to males aged 65–9 was 53 : 47. In the 70–4 age group, the ratio was 56 females to 44 males, whilst, for the over 75s, the ratio was 62 : 38 (OPCS 1994*b*). Women form a larger majority the greater the chronological age within old age. This is because women have longer life expectancies than men. The faster reduction in female than male mortality has resulted in what Arber and Ginn (1991) term the 'feminization of later life' (Table 6.2).

Table 6.2 Expectation of life at birth for women and men, United Kingdom, 1906–1994

	Women	Men	Difference
1906	52	48	4
1944	67	62	5
1994	79	73	6

Sources: Arber and Ginn 1991; Central Statistical Office 1994a.

The preponderance of women is one aspect of the 'gendered process' (Arber and Ginn 1991) of old age. A second aspect is the significant differences in the experiences of men and women within old age. Ageism and sexism combine together, with the result that women are at a far greater disadvantage than men as they grow old. For example, negative attitudes to old age are far more pronounced for women than they are for men. Arber and Ginn discuss evidence, such as the depiction of old women in children's stories as 'evil old hags' and the persecution of old women as witches in fifteenth- and sixteenth-century Europe, which leads them to conclude that 'older women have been at the sharp end of misogyny throughout the history of patriarchal societies' (1991: 40). Arber and Ginn also point to such tendencies in contemporary society, where older women are, more commonly than men, characterized as slow, stupid, unhealthy, unattractive, and dependent (1991: 41). Sontag (1979) argues that there is a 'double standard of ageing', one for women and one for men. The qualities and attributes that women are valued for, namely their youthful physical attractiveness, do not stand up well to age. Men's value, Sontag argues, depends less on how they look and more on what they do. Sontag also points to the ways in which signs of ageing on men are less heavily penalized than they are on women. In fact, wrinkles and greying hair on men are likely to be taken as a sign of character and to be described as 'distinguished'. Women are under more pressure to 'ward off signs of ageing' than men, in part due to the extent to which women's sexual candidacy is dependent upon their physical attractiveness (Sontag 1979). British sociologist Catherine Itzin (cited in Arber and Ginn 1991) offers a similar analysis. She argues that there are gendered 'chronologies', one for women and one for men. Whilst male chronology hinges on employment, Itzin argues that a woman's age status is defined in terms of events in the reproductive cycle. Women are, consequently, valued highly in the earlier part of their life courses, when they are attractive, available, and useful to men. It follows that, in later life, women's 'value' and status decline earlier and more sharply than men's. A familiar example of the 'double standard' of ageing is the greater disapproval shown toward a sexual relationship between an older woman and a younger man, than is the case vice versa.

Ageism and sexism also combine together to the extent that there are significant *material effects* of the 'double standard' which, once again, mean that older women are at a greater disadvantage than older men. Although, as indicated earlier, many old people are at risk of poverty, women are at far greater risk of poverty within old age than men. As Groves (1993) argues, this is directly related to the earlier life course histories of women and men, for example, in their different opportunities to carry out paid work. An individual's employment career (and that of his or her partner) is of crucial importance in determining the adequacy of material resources in later life. Women's employment opportunities have been, and continue to be, more restricted than men's. This means that women are less likely to be eligible for a state pension in their own right and are less likely to have built up savings or investments, due to their intermittent employment histories. Groves notes that income from employers or occupational pensions is the key to living above the poverty line in old age, but that women aged 65 and over are far less likely to have one than are men aged 65 and over. Ginn and Arber (1992) also argue that the major reason for gender differences in income in old age arises from women's lesser entitlement to occupational and private pensions.

In later life and old age, access to resources essential to retain independence is profoundly influenced by earlier life histories, particularly in relation to employment. The work histories of the current cohort of elderly women mean that they suffer from lower income levels in old age and are at greater risk from poverty. Although it is clear that sexism and ageism combine to create a 'double jeopardy' (Itzin 1984) for old women in contemporary society, cohort processes may alter the experience of later life for women in the future. Arber and Ginn (1991) suggest that future cohorts of older women, influenced by feminism and with longer education and careers, will demand a 'better deal' as they age and claim the right to age without stigma. Certainly, recent data indicates that future cohorts of elderly women are more likely to have income from an occupational or personal pension in their old age. In 1992, 74 per cent of female full-time employees aged 55 and over were members of an occupation or personal pension scheme, compared with 85 per cent of those aged 35–44. However, it should be noted that whilst 75 per cent of all female full-time employees were members of an occupational or personal pension scheme, only 32 per cent of all female part-time employees were. Moreover, men are still more likely than women to be members of such a scheme (OPCS 1994*b*).

Gender and cohort, then, make a difference to the experience of old age. The same is also true of ethnicity. The age structure of the British population varies by ethnic group. Only 3 per cent of the ethnic minority population are aged 65 and over, compared with 17 per cent of the white population (OPCS 1993*a*). The ethnic minority population has a young age structure, reflecting the history of immigration to Britain, particularly in the 1950s and 1960s. The proportion of ethnic minority elderly people will increase in the future, as the ethnic minority population itself ages. For current cohorts, inequalities in income and health between ethnic groups have been shown to increase with age. There are also distinct differences in residence patterns, with older Asians in particular rarely living on their own (Blakemore 1989).

This chapter has shown that old age is a stage in the life course in modern Britain with relatively low status. 'Old' is a stigmatized social identity. This is largely a result of the economic marginalization of old people, which means that many of them have low levels of income and are at great risk of poverty. Experiences in later life and old age, though, are very much determined by the earlier life course experiences of individuals, particularly their employment histories. This means that working-class people, women, and members of ethnic minority groups are more likely to suffer prejudice and disadvantage in their old age.

Older people then, are not uniformly disadvantaged and powerless. Hockey and James argue that, although old people are a marginalized category, individuals may nevertheless draw on and mobilize one or more of three sources of power, depending on their social position

(1993: 159). The first source of power arises from advantage conferred through wealth and/or social status, including class, gender, and ethnicity. This means that individuals can ameliorate or even transcend the disadvantages of old age through drawing on such sources of power. White, well-off males are in a particularly advantageous position in this respect. The second source of power identified by Hockey and James is that arising from *resistance* to the imposition of a category or label which is damaging to an individual's status. Evidence from the Thompson *et al.* (1991) study shows that chronologically old people disassociate themselves from the stigmatized social identity of 'old'. Another study showed that, among elderly people living in residential care, some take on the role of carer to others more ill and frail than themselves. Hockey and James argue that such a strategy grants the elderly person as carer, 'a fragile and transitory membership of the more powerful social category "able-bodied adult"' (1993: 166). The third source of power arises from *visible* membership of a disadvantaged social category. On an individual level, elderly people subjected to the infantilization practices of more powerful adults (see Chapter Five), may deliberately act as if they were children as a form of resistance and, in so doing, retain an element of control in their interactions with adults. On a collective level, there are indications of an increasingly politicized 'age-consciousness' amongst elderly people (Milne 1994). This represents an assertion of membership of a negatively perceived category (old people), with an aim of ultimately improving its status (Hockey and James 1993: 171). Currently, the political organization of old people in order to protect and promote their interests is more advanced in America than in Britain. In America, the Grey Panthers campaign against ageism and have influenced policy and laws relating to older people. In Britain in the 1990s, we can only really speak of an emerging 'grey movement'. Nevertheless, organizations such as the National Federation of Retirement Pensioners' Association, the Pensioners' Rights Campaign, and the Association of Retired Persons Over 50 have a probable combined membership of over 100,000. The extent to which old people become a political force to be reckoned with, especially in the light of the further ageing of the population in the twenty-first century, remains to be seen.

Further Reading

Like the studies of Thompson (1992) and colleagues (1991), Williams's (1990) study of elderly Scots uses the words of people themselves to describe the experience of old age. Networks of support amongst the elderly in rural Wales have been studied by Wenger (1994). Blakemore and Boneham (1994) report on black and Asian elderly people in Britain, drawing comparisons with the USA and Australia, whilst Hugman (1994) examines old age in various European countries. For political activity amongst older people, *Critical Social Policy* (No. 18, Winter 1986–7) contains useful articles which report on the American Grey Panthers as well as the British 'grey movement'.

Chapter Seven

Give and Take?
Age Relationships and the
Transfer of Support

In previous chapters, which have considered successive stages of the life course from childhood to old age, the issue of relationships between people of different ages has been an important subtheme. For example, it has been stressed several times that the life course is best understood as a cumulative and interconnected process. This involves recognition of the interrelationships between the life courses of *different* individuals, as well as between stages within any one individual's life course. For one's own position in the life course is, at least in part, indicated by the nature and intensity of relationships with individuals who are at particular stages of their own life course. 'Children' are persons whose position in the life course is defined in relation to their parents' life course stage (and, to a lesser extent, vice versa). Chapter Three showed how relationships between children and parents, as occupants of two different but connected stages of the life course, are marked by inequalities in power and access to resources. A characteristic of youth as a stage in the life course is the nature and intensity of relationships with peer groups, with persons of the same life course stage, expressed in the form of youth cultures. One of the markers of adulthood evident in cultural practices in modern Britain, is the completion of the transition from family of origin (usually the parental home) to an independent household. In turn, middle age as a stage in the life course is marked, for some people, by their children leaving home. Becoming a grandparent to your child's child provides a further example of how one's own position in the life course is in part indicated by the relationships one has with persons who are at a different stage of their life course. The examples given here are mainly those where an individual's life course stage is indicated by their *kinship* relationships with persons of a different life course stage. Hareven (1982*b*) terms this element of life course processes 'family time', one of three 'levels' of time within the life course (see Chapter Two). Family time refers to the transitions individuals make into different family or kinship roles as families themselves grow 'older'. Of course, as they move through their life course, individuals also engage in relationships with persons, occupying different life course positions to themselves, who are not their kin. Within the education system, for example, children (as pupils) are taught by and are subject to the authority of adults (as teachers). Frail, elderly people in hospitals or in residential homes are cared for by persons who are invariably at an earlier life course stage than themselves. Relationships between individuals in the adult world of employment, and elsewhere in society, are very heterogeneous in terms of the mix of individuals at different stages of the life course, although in employment children and old people tend to be excluded.

As was explained in Chapter One, stage in life course is one aspect of the ageing process. 'Age', counted (at least in Western cultures) chronologically from date of birth, is also made up of *physiological* ageing processes and *cohort* processes. Individuals who are children, young people, adults, or old, who are the occupants of different life course stages *at one point in time*, are also likely to differ in their chronological age, their physiological age, and in their cohort membership. Previous chapters have noted the importance in modern Britain of chronological age, in terms of its official function of compelling, prohibiting, or permitting persons to undertake certain activities. In this way, chronological age acts to shape age relationships, empowering some individuals and disempowering others. Previous chapters have also considered the role an individual's *body* plays as a signifier of age-based social status, particularly to persons with younger or older bodies. In Chapter Six, the argument of Dowd (1986), who lays emphasis on the role of cohort processes in shaping age relationships, was presented. For younger cohorts, older cohorts are stigmatized due to their (perceived) antiquated cultural preferences: the old are 'old fashioned' and have 'past-situated' social identities.

Although it is a theme which has been largely implicit, the evidence presented in the previous chapters has, in the ways indicated above, been very much about age relationships, particularly in terms of inequalities of power, status, and access to resources that exist between persons of different ages; and transitions in personal relationships with individuals of different ages, that are part of the experience of growing up and growing older. Within this chapter, though, the issue of age relationships takes centre stage.

'Generation' is the everyday term used when reference is made to relationships between individuals and groups of different ages, as in 'the generation gap'. 'Generational' relationships, as popularly conceived, take place on two different levels and between two to three broad 'generations'. On the family level, 'generational' relationships take place between children/young people, parents, and grandparents. On a societal level, 'generational' relationships are commonly perceived to take place between children/young people, adults (of working age) and (retired) old age pensioners; or even just between 'the young' and 'the old' in a rather vague and ill-defined categorization. This chapter draws on evidence and debates relating to both 'levels' of 'generational' relationships, although the terminology applied to describe relationships at the societal level differs. (As noted at the outset of this book, 'generation' is, properly, a structural term which denotes kinship relationships and its usage should be restricted to this meaning). Beginning with a focus on intergenerational relationships in terms of 'give and take' between family and kin, the chapter then considers similar relationships between people of different age groupings that take place at the societal level, namely between, on the one hand, persons of working age and, on the other, young and old persons who are 'dependent'. Here, the issue of the 'dependency ratio' is examined in the context of the ageing of the population, and the matter of 'justice over time' (Laslett and Fishkin 1992) is considered.

Intergenerational Relationships

As Finch puts it, 'Age and generational position are important in families almost by definition' (1989: 53). An individual's family is likely to be made up of some combination of the following: a sexual partner, parents, children, grandparents, uncles, aunts, siblings. In this section, the focus of attention is on the transfer of support and resources between generations within kinship groups, namely between parents, children, and grandchildren. Finch defines kin groups as adults who are related through blood or marriage, or who are treated as if they were so related (1989: 3). Here, I consider kin relationships between generations which include children as well as adults. First, a brief survey of historical evidence is undertaken, which, amongst other things, underlines the relatively recent emergence of multi-generational families. Second, evidence on the extent and nature of supportive relationships within kin groups in modern Britain is reviewed. Finch (1989) has drawn together evidence in both these areas in a comprehensive and admirable way; the following account draws heavily on her work.

Intergenerational Relationships in History

Having reviewed historical evidence on support between kin, Finch describes the belief that family responsibilities were stronger in the past than they are today as 'mythical'. One aspect of this myth is the belief that there was a greater prevalence of extended family households in the pre-industrial past. This way of living was thought to have provided the opportunity for intensive intergenerational relationships. However, more recent historical research has shown that extended family households existed only for a minority of people. Household structures aside, there is no evidence that people assumed automatic responsibility for their kin who were incapacitated through illness or old age. Rather, the evidence suggests that patterns of support between the generations operated on a basis of 'mutual advantage' (Finch 1989: 65). As shown in Chapter Six, for example, the needs of people in their old age were more likely to be attended to if they had material resources. In addition, old people were more likely to be taken into the household of a relative if they could offer services, such as child care or housework, in exchange.

Although pre-industrial society was not a golden age in terms of intergenerational relationships, processes of change linked to industrialization clearly had an impact on the extent and nature of intergenerational support. As shown in Chapters Three and Four, children and young people had important economic roles in pre-industrial and early industrial society. Gillis (1974) has described how, in pre-industrial society, the apprenticeship system meant that children left home from the age of 7 or thereabouts to live in other households, as servants or apprentices for a trade. Processes linked to industrialization transformed the lives of these young people, tying them closer to their families, as they began to remain at home until their marriage. Other writers have suggested that the growth in wage labour meant that there was a real advantage in keeping as many children of working age at home as possible. Gittins (1993), for example, argues that this development must have had important repercussions on power relationships between the generations. There was bound to be pressure on children not to marry and leave home, since their earnings represented an important part of the household's total income. By the end of the nineteenth century, employment and education legislation had restricted the economic contribution children and young people could make to their families, and hence the nature of the relationship between them and their parents had undergone change. Childhood and youth were established as stages of the life course characterized by a largely one-way dependency, of children and young people on their parents. Old people, as we have seen were similarly excluded from the labour market. However, the provision of old age pensions has meant that old people have been able to obtain a degree of financial independence from younger generations of their kin. Finch suggests, then, that changes over time in patterns of support between generations are shaped in important ways by economic conditions, legislation, and social policy (1989: 71–4).

Demographic factors have also affected patterns of intergenerational relationships over time. Statistical evidence shows that, in the pre-modern past, high rates of mortality meant that relatively few people could expect to reach 'old age' (age 65) and even fewer could expect to enjoy a lengthy old age. This had implications for the overlap of generations within families, and, therefore, for the very possibility of there being intergenerational relationships. However, as Anderson (1985) shows, demographic changes before and during the twentieth century have affected both the possibility of and duration of overlaps between the generations. Anderson provides the following example of the impact of demographic changes. He writes that, 'in the 1970s, an average woman could expect to live for 14 years longer than a similar woman in the early eighteenth century. But her age at the marriage of her last child had fallen by some 13 years and her age at the birth of her last grandchild by about 22 years . . .' (1985: 74). Whilst an average woman of the mid-eighteenth century could expect to *die* twelve years *before* her last grandchild was born, a woman of the 1970s could expect to *live* twenty-five years *after* the birth of her last grandchild (1985: 70). Such changes over the centuries meant that grandparents of the inter-war years were the first of whom a majority would know all their grand-children. By the 1970s, even men could expect to live long enough to see all their grandchildren married, assuming that they married at the average age (1985: 75).

There are two main sets of demographic factors which have brought about an increased likelihood of families with three generations of adults, and, therefore, of a lengthy duration of intergenerational rela-tionships. First, a decrease in mortality rates has meant that more indi-viduals survive to reach old age. Second, changes have taken place in patterns of childrearing, brought about by the decrease in fertility rates and a related clustering of children into the early years of marriage. This has meant that most children have been born to 'young' parents, who in turn become 'young' grandparents as the pattern is repeated across the generations. Finch (1989) concludes that the coexistence of three adult generations over a long period of time creates opportunities for a wider range of intergenerational support and resource transfers.

Intergenerational Relationships in Modern Britain

Demographic changes have resulted in the coexistence of three adult generations over a lengthy period of time, opening up the *possibility* of a range of intergenerational relationships involving support and resources. What does the evidence show about the nature and extent of these relationships in modern Britain? Finch reviews a range of evidence which leads her to argue that assistance from relatives is of considerable importance to many people. She identifies five types of support that generations provide for each other (1989: 15–36).

Economic support. This type of support includes giving or lending money, providing gifts of food or clothing, leaving economic assets to kin via a will after death, and finding employment. Finch concludes that the common pattern is one of an uneven flow of support across the generations, with more flowing from those older to those younger. This uneven flow continues throughout the life course and beyond, via inheritance bequeathed to younger generations. Economic support of children by parents is most intensive and complete for children under 16 years of age. They provide somewhere to live, food, clothing, and so on. Parents also give children pocket-money although this form of economic support is likely to be gradually withdrawn when children begin to earn their own money from part-time employment. Older children remaining in the parental home who are in employment or receiving another form of independent income, such as a student grant or state benefit, are likely to pay 'board money' to their parents, in exchange for the provision of accommodation and food (Wallace 1987). Where a young person is unemployed, this form of intergenerational exchange may operate largely at the symbolic level (Hutson and Jenkins 1989).

Accommodation. Most children under the age of 16 live with their parents. Data from the Scottish Young Peoples' Survey shows that even at age 19, around 75 per cent of males and 68 per cent of females live in their parental home (Jones and Wallace 1992). A sizeable minority of the population live with parents as couples, especially those young people who cohabit or marry at a relatively young age. A third form of intergenerational sharing of accommodation is where elderly people live with their relatives. This is quite rare; only 6 per cent of people aged 65 and over lived with their children in 1991 (OPCS 1994c). However, it is more common for older Asian people to live with their relatives (Blakemore and Boneham 1994). A fourth example is where adult children return to live with their parents, following marital breakdown and divorce. This arrangement is generally regarded as a temporary one. Again, in the case of intergenerational support involving accommodation, the tendency is for the older generation to provide support to the younger generation.

Personal care. For Finch, this type of support refers to nursing care and/or performing domestic work for those adult kin who are ill, disabled, or elderly. Here, the evidence reviewed by Finch suggests that women provide the great majority of personal care to relatives and that the parent–child relationship is the next most important source of support after the spouse relationship. Children, mainly daughters, are a major source of support for elderly parents. Parents, mainly mothers, are the principal supporters of adult disabled children. Under this category of support, the personal care of dependent children by their parents can also be included. In Western cultures, young children in particular are perceived to need high levels of personal care. This gradually reduces over time as the child is perceived to be increasingly able to care for itself. Again, studies show that it is mothers who are most likely to provide personal care to their children. Where children have sick or disabled parents, they may act as important providers of personal care. Overall, the evidence suggests that the nature and extent of personal care between the generations varies across the life course. Extensive amounts of support are provided by older to younger generations in the early part of the younger generation's life course. Extensive support is also given by younger to older during the later part of the older generation's life course. It is possible that people view the care given to their children as being reciprocated at a later point, when their children care for them in their old age (although, see evidence from Finch and Mason 1993, discussed shortly).

Practical support. For Finch, this type of support refers to activities such as doing each other's washing or shopping, but particularly, providing child care. A recent government survey found that grandparents are the most likely carers for pre-school children with working parents, with 23 per cent of such children being regularly looked after by their grandparents (OPCS 1994d). Other evidence suggests that within this type of intergenerational support, it is grandmothers, rather than grandfathers, who are likely to be the active carer. In general, this type of support is highly gendered, flowing mainly from and between women kin. The direction of flow again tends to be from older to younger generations. Children living in the parental home may, though, undertake household chores and those with younger siblings may act as their parents' 'baby-sitters'.

Emotional and moral support. This type of support, as identified by Finch, refers to listening, talking, and giving advice, both in a routine way and at times of crisis. Evidence reviewed by Finch suggests, for example, that mothers of small children turn to their own mothers for advice about their children's health. Younger generations may also seek advice from older generations about finances or large purchases. Jones and Wallace (1992) argue that parents advise their children on moves linked to the transition to adulthood, such as whether to stay on at school, although Brown (1990) suggests that recent changes in education to employment transitions have led to 'generational discontinuity' in this respect. The stock of cultural knowledge which parents previously passed on may no longer be as relevant. As with other types of support, emotional and moral support appears to be gendered and largely one-way in the flow from older to younger generations. Overall, the evidence on this type of support seems less clear-cut. It seems likely that, as individuals grow older their main source of emotional support may well lie outside their family, with friends for example (O'Connor 1991).

In summary, then, Finch's perusal of the research evidence on the nature and extent of intergenerational support shows that it takes place to a significant extent and takes a variety of forms. The coexistence of three generations of adults in families is, as noted above, a fairly recent phenomenon. Whilst evidence underlines the importance of

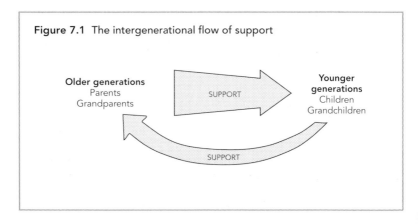

Figure 7.1 The intergenerational flow of support

Older generations
Parents
Grandparents

SUPPORT

Younger generations
Children
Grandchildren

SUPPORT

parent–child relationships throughout the life course, knowledge about grandparent–grandchild relationships is lacking. This is particularly true where the grandchild is an adult. Finch (1989) notes an empirical problem in understanding how support operates between grandparents and grandchildren, in that it is difficult to disentangle it from support given to and by the middle generation. For example, when a grandparent provides child care or clothes for grandchildren, it is unclear whether support is in fact being given to their children, rather than to their grandchildren. Empirical difficulties aside, what the limited available evidence does show is that grandparenthood is welcomed (Cotterill 1992) and that relationships with grandchildren are valued highly. Given that evidence shows that support seems normally to flow from older to younger generations, we might expect this also to be the case in grandparent–grandchild relationships. As Finch (1989: 55) puts it, 'Parents give to their children and their grandchildren and continue to give' (Figure 7.1). This interpretation is confirmed by Finch's later empirical study of family responsibilities (Finch and Mason 1993). Parent to child transfers of support were found to dominate, including in terms of financial assistance, providing a home, and looking after grandchildren. Transfers of support *were* found to flow the other way (from children to parents) but mainly in the form of practical help given, such as shopping and cleaning, and in providing personal care. Finch and Mason's study also examined people's ideas about the extent and nature of support that should flow between the generations. The highest level of agreement amongst the sample was in response to a statement concerning a young couple returning home from abroad and having nowhere to live. Around 86 per cent of the respondents said that relatives should offer the couple a temporary home. Finch and Mason also found a high degree of consensus (79 per cent) on the advisability of a newly homeless 19-year-old mother returning to her parental home. These examples indicate high levels of consensus as to support which should flow from older to younger generations. In contrast, only 27 per cent of the sample said that a frail and immobile old person, no longer able to live alone, should move in with relatives. Over half the sample (55 per cent) said that she or he should move into an old people's home. A related finding was that 39 per cent of the sample said children do not have an obligation to look after their parents when they are old (58 per cent said children do have an obligation). Finch and Mason's (1993) study shows, then, that there was more agreement about the assistance that should be given to younger generations than to older generations.

Recent government policies have been concerned, in various ways, to encourage families to support their kin rather than the state. Chapter Four described the various reductions in young people's eligibility for state benefits, including student grants and housing benefit. It was argued that these changes can be interpreted as attempts to transfer responsibility for the material provision of young people on to their families. Government policy toward child care (that is, no state provision) and the establishment of the Child Support Agency, can also be interpreted as attempts to encourage older generations within families to materially provide for younger generations, rather than their needs being met by the state.

This account of intergenerational relationships has drawn heavily on Finch (1989). The importance of Finch's work lies in her argument that the support given to people by their relatives is not just a matter of preferences and choices, but is governed to a considerable extent by the prevailing social, economic, and demographic conditions of the time, including in terms of the emphasis of government policy. These are important points to keep in mind as the focus of attention moves now to questions of 'dependency ratios' and the ageing of the population.

Transfer of Resources at the Societal Level

As has been argued in previous chapters, certain stages of the life course in modern Britain, especially childhood and old age, are conceptualized and constructed as *dependent* stages. Other stages, especially adulthood, are conceptualized and constructed as *independent* stages. Hockey and James (1993) propose that this process should be understood as a consequence of the material and symbolic importance of work or employment in modern Britain. This means that those who participate in the labour market have high social status (are independent), while those who are marginally involved in the labour market have low social status (are dependent).

Individuals within the dependent stage of *childhood* have limited direct access to resources, especially income from paid work. Their material needs are, in most cases, provided for them by their parents. In the absence of parental provision, the state acts in place of parents to meet the material needs of children. It is through material support given to children, mainly by their parents but also by the state, that children can continue to be only marginally involved in the labour market and, hence, a dependent category of persons. Children in modern Britain generally do not *have* to work in order to survive, even if they might wish to or were legally able to. In addition to children's material needs being met, in most cases, by parents (supported by the state in the form of Child Benefit), their educational 'needs' are provided for by the state education system. At least up until age 16, children are guaranteed free, full-time education. The health needs of children are also provided for by the state, via the National Health Service, under which they are one of a few categories of persons to receive completely free treatment.

Old age is the other main stage of the life course which is conceptualized and constructed as dependent. Unlike children, individuals who are old, in most cases, do not have parents to materially provide for them. Moreover, we have seen that only a small proportion of people aged 65 and over live with their children. Most old people, either live alone or with their spouse (Box 6.1). In this sense, old people are more independent than are children or young people. Data have been presented which show that the great majority of people aged 65 and over live in households where no one is in employment, and that, in households where the head is aged 65 and over, around half of the household income comes from social security benefits, including the state pension (Chapter Six). From this evidence, it is clear that the welfare state provides old people with a significant amount of material support, enabling them to retire from full-time employment at age 60 or 65, even though they may be physically capable of remaining at work and thus materially providing for themselves. Although the state does not provide for the educational needs of old people to the extent it does for children, their health care needs are met (on the whole) by the National Health Service and some of their personal care needs are met through locally provided social services (such as Meals on Wheels and Home Help).

From the above discussion, the welfare state emerges as the agency which in the case of children and young people facilitates their dependency, and in the case of old people is the mainstay of their dependency. The welfare state is most often conceived of as an institution which distributes resources between the wealthy, the relatively wealthy, and the poor. Clearly, it does fulfil this function, at least to a degree. Several writers, though, have argued for the welfare state to be analysed, in addition, as an institution which distributes resources between individuals of different *ages*. Certainly, from the above discussion, the welfare state can be seen to distribute resources to the young and the old. If these categories of persons are the *receivers*, who then are the *contributors*? In simple terms, it is the economically active adult population who, via the various taxes that they pay, provide the major 'input' into the welfare system, so supporting the dependency of children and old people, amongst others.

When a population remains stable over time, in that the distribution of age groups within it remains fairly constant, then the system of redistributing resources between persons of different ages seems a relatively just, uncontentious one. Although recipients when young, individuals, eventually and for a lengthy period, become contributors during their economically active adult life. On retirement, individuals become recipients once more during their old age. Over time, then, individuals give to and take from the system in proportion. Difficulty arises, however, when the age structure alters over time, particularly when there are relatively more persons in dependent categories and fewer persons in non-dependent categories. As was shown in Chapter One, Britain is undergoing such an alteration in age structure. The scenario is one of a greater number of recipients relying on a smaller number of contributors, who may, as a consequence, be required to give proportionately more of their earnings.

The proportion of dependent categories of persons to non-dependent categories of persons in the economy is most often expressed as the *dependency ratio*. This is calculated as the number of individuals in the non-economically active population divided by the number of individuals in the economically active population. The most widely used definitions here are those under school leaving age (0–15) plus those over retirement age (60/65), divided by the population of working age (16–59/64). As Table 7.1 shows, during the twentieth century, the dependency ratio has increased and is projected to increase further during the twenty-first century. The worsening dependency ratio is mainly a consequence of the ageing of the population, as older people make up an increasingly larger proportion of the total population over time. In 1901, there were 12 elderly people per 100 of the population of working age. By the year 2031, it is projected that there will be 48 elderly people per 100 of the population of working age (Table 7.1). At the same time, the proportion of the population of working age is predicted to shrink, from 61 per cent in 1991 to 56 per cent in 2031 (Johnson and Falkingham 1992). The change in the age structure is a consequence of fluctuations in the size of birth cohorts during the twentieth century. The relatively large birth cohort of the 1950s and 1960s (the 'baby boomers') are currently at the economically active stage of their life courses. The welfare system, including the state pension system and the National Health Service, operates on a 'pay-as-you-go' basis. Contributions currently paid into the system by today's workers are simultaneously redistributed to today's dependants. In

Table 7.1 Number of dependants per 100 population of working age, 1901–2031

	1901	1951	1992	2031[c]
Elderly people[a]	12	21	30	48
Children[b]		36	33	33
Total dependants		37	63	80

[a] Defined as those of pensionable age
[b] Defined as those under school leaving age
[c] Projected on the basis of women retiring at age 60 and men at 65

Sources: Johnson and Falkingham 1992; OPCS 1994a; Central Statistical Office 1994a.

contemporary Britain, it is the contributions of the relatively large cohort of economically active age which supports the welfare state, on which old people are particularly reliant.

So far, this system has worked rather well. However, the large 'baby boom' cohort has been followed by a relatively small birth cohort (which some writers have termed 'the baby bust'). This means that when the 'baby boomers' become elderly, they will be reliant on the 'inputs' made to the welfare system by a significantly smaller cohort of working age. Under such changed demographic conditions, the fairness or 'justice over time' of the distribution of societal resources between age groups becomes problematical. The personal and health care costs, pensions, and other social security benefit costs which are likely to accompany the ageing of the population, it is feared, will place an unsustainable burden on the population of working age. In the future, younger, smaller cohorts of workers may not be able, or willing, to support a larger cohort of old age dependants. The situation has been described by some as 'the demographic time bomb'. In America, anxiety is such that a pressure group has been established to push for justice and equity in the distribution of resources between age groups. In the face of the ageing of the population and what they see as the 'greying' of the federal budget, 'Americans for Generational Equity' argue against directing resources to the elderly and maintain instead that they should be directed at children and the young. In Britain, too, as elsewhere in the Western industrialized world, the predicted worsening of the dependency ratio is viewed by many with considerable alarm. In the light of the ageing of the population and the worsening dependency ratio, writers like Arber and Ginn (1991) detect a growth in a more politicized ageism in Britain, where the elderly are scapegoated as voracious consumers of scarce societal resources and are portrayed as placing an unsustainable burden on the rest of the population.

   In assessing arguments about the impact of the ageing of the population, in terms of a worsening dependency ratio and the sustainability of the burden placed on the population of working age, there are a number of points to consider. First, the way in which the dependency ratio is conventionally calculated has been criticized. As explained above, the dependency ratio is most often calculated as the population under school leaving age plus those over retirement age, divided by those of working age. Here, it is age alone which defines whether or not a person is 'dependent'. As Johnson and Falkingham (1992) point out, changes in the structure of the labour market and in labour force participation rates over the last few decades have considerably weakened the validity of distinguishing between 'dependent' and 'worker' on the grounds of age alone. Earlier, in Chapter Four, changes to the employment participation rates of young people were described. Survey evidence was presented which showed that under half of 16–18-year-olds and just over half of 18–19-year-olds were in employment in 1990/1. Changes to 'workending' were discussed in Chapter Five and evidence here indicated that only 62 per cent of men aged 60–4 were economically active in 1992. These data on labour market participation rates amongst young people and older people show that age 16 to 64 is not a reliable indicator of 'worker' status. Calculations using age as the criterion can be seen to *underestimate* the ratio of dependants to non-dependants in the economy. Falkingham (1989) argues that the 'engine of dependency' has at least two other 'cylinders', namely patterns of labour force participation across age and gender and levels of unemployment. She suggests that economic activity status, rather than age, be used in the calculation of dependency ratios. When this more sensitive measure is used, the overall level of dependency is at present higher than is usually recognized. Since this has been accommodated, Falkingham suggests, a similar accommodation may well be made in the future.

   A second point to consider is this. Even if age-based measures of dependency are used, it has been suggested that the rise in the number of elderly dependants has been and will be offset, to some extent, by a fall in the proportion of young dependants. A smaller child and young adult population may be accompanied by a reduced education budget and reduced expenditure on Child Benefit, for example, therefore allowing an increase in spending to meet the needs of the elderly population. However, Johnson and Falkingham (1992) argue against treating dependent categories of persons as interchangeable with one another. They point out that the total public costs of support for people aged 65 and over is considerably more than public costs of support for children under 16. Furthermore, elderly people 'cost' more in welfare expenditure terms the older they are. Between 1992 and 2032, the proportions of the population aged 75–84 and 85 and over is projected to rise by 51 per cent and 126 per cent respectively (OPCS 1994a). It is clear that numbers of elderly and very elderly people are set to increase in the future. Yet, it would be unwise to make blanket assumptions about their material and health needs. The importance of not treating 'old people' as a homogeneous category was illustrated in Chapter Six. Not every individual within future cohorts of the elderly will be equally dependent upon the state. Significant differences in access to financial and material resources, health resources, and domestic/caring resources (Arber and Ginn 1991) shown to exist within old age are likely to persist into the future. Furthermore, Thane (1989) reminds us that the health of future elderly people cannot be predicted with any certainty because health and illness are subject to social definitions and are likely to be affected by a cohort's earlier life experiences. Correspondingly, the future personal care and health care 'costs' of the elderly cannot be predicted with any certainty.

A third point that needs to be taken into account in the assessment of arguments surrounding worsening dependency ratios, and their consequences, is that dependency in old age is *socially* constructed. Accordingly, the proportion of elderly dependants in the population can fluctuate as a consequence of social practices and government policies. This point is illustrated by government plans to equalize the retirement age by the year 2010. At this time, both women and men will retire and become eligible for a state pension at age 65 (Wintour 1993). All the calculations as to future dependency ratios and the assumptions as to the consequences, have been made on the basis that women will continue to retire and become eligible for a state pension at age 60. The planned change to the retirement age for women will mean that dependency ratios (as conventionally calculated) will improve, if only slightly: women will, after 2010, remain non-dependants for longer than has previously been assumed. Countries like Denmark, Sweden, and Norway have plans to raise their retirement age to 67, in the face of their ageing population and concerns about dependency ratios (Wintour 1993). The size of dependent populations and non-dependent populations can, then, be changed by legislation and the operation of state welfare policies.

A final point to consider is that concerns about the dependency ratio and the 'burden' of the ageing population have arisen during a period of adverse economic conditions and at a time when government attitudes toward the welfare state have become hostile (Walker and Phillipson 1986). The system of distributing societal resources between dependants and non-dependants through the welfare state worked reasonably well and was favoured by successive governments up until the 1970s, when the economic and political climate changed. In the future, improved economic conditions and a change in governmental attitudes towards the welfare state may lead to a reduction in concerns about the 'burden' of the elderly population. To conclude, most arguments about the worsening dependency ratio, the demographic time bomb, and future conflict over the distribution of resources employ a crude 'demographic determinism'. Future trends concerning 'dependants' and 'workers' have at least as much to do with economic conditions, patterns of labour force participation, and the operation of social policy as they have to do with demographics. In the words of Johnson and Falkingham (1992: 47), and as the above analysis suggests, 'the alarmist views on population ageing may prove unfounded and the true picture certainly more complex'.

Those readers who are in any way familiar with the debates featured in the latter part of this chapter will have noticed that certain terms, more usually employed when such issues are discussed, have been absent. Earlier in this book, a case was made for restricting the use of generational terms to the discussion of kinship relations. Hence, in setting out arguments concerning the ageing of the population and the dependency ratio, I have deliberately avoided phrases such as 'generational equity', 'intergenerational transfers', or 'conflict between the generations'. Clearly, the ageing of the population and the management of the dependency of large numbers of elderly people has implications for kin relationships. This is particularly so in the light of government policy aimed at encouraging families to 'take care of their own', rather than relying on the state to do so. However, the issue of the implications of an ageing population for kin relationships needs to be separated out from the issue of the ways in which the dependency of large numbers of elderly people is managed at *societal* level. To use generational terminology to refer to both 'levels' of relationships is unhelpful. The transfer of resources between age groups that takes place through the taxation system via the welfare state is best conceptualized as transfers between individuals at different stages of the *life course*. Thinking about these issues from the life course perspective has several advantages. It encourages full recognition of the ways in which dependent status associated with particular stages of the life course is *socially* constructed. In other words, it heightens our awareness that the dependency of old people is the direct outcome of social and cultural practices, including political and economic policies, which are subject to change. A life course perspective also encourages a recognition of the ways in which an individual occupies both dependent and independent statuses at different points within his or her life course. Cole (1989) argues that bringing a life course perspective to bear on the debate about population ageing and altered dependency ratios encourages a degree of solidarity between age groups, whereas concepts like 'generation' are divisive. A life course perspective emphasizes the fact that individuals occupy a variety of age-based social statuses over time: the elderly are not some separate entity, but are our future selves. A further advantage of the life course perspective arises from its recognition of the importance of cohort. Clearly, cohort processes are directly relevant to discussions of the changing dependency ratio. It is the unevenness in the size of cohorts at different stages of the life course that has led to concerns about the management of the dependency of elderly people in the future. This issue of cohort size and the way it impacts upon people's experiences and opportunities is considered further in the following chapter, as the focus of attention now shifts to the importance of cohort membership.

Further Reading

A collection edited by Brannen and Wilson (1987) provides evidence on the distribution of resources within households. Wenger (1984) includes data on contact with and support from children and grandchildren amongst elderly people. Johnson and Falkingham (1992) is an up-to-date, detailed examination of the issues raised by the ageing population. The volume edited by Laslett and Fishkin (1992) includes contributions which, as well as the distribution of welfare resources, consider the issue of 'justice over time' between cohorts in relation to the environment, and compensation paid to present cohorts for wrong-doings committed against their ancestors.

Chapter Eight

Cohort Membership

A cohort is a grouping of individuals who share the same significant event, especially their birth, at or within a given period of time. Such a cohort may be narrowly defined (individuals born on the same day, or in the same month, or year) or more broadly defined (individuals born, say, within a five- or ten-year period). As a concept, cohort contextualizes the life course of an individual in two main ways. First, it serves to locate a life course within a specific period of historical time. As explained in Chapter One, in Western cultures age is counted in calendar time. A person who is of a particular numerical age is always a person who has lived through a particular slice of history. The cohort to which an individual belongs, by virtue of date of birth and death, acts to shape the range and possibilities of experiences open to him or her. Second, the concept of cohort serves to place the life courses of individuals in the context of the lives of their fellow cohort members, that is, those who are of the same or similar calendar age. Cohort members are those who are born and grow up and older more or less in tandem with each other. Consequently, cohort members share a common exposure to certain experiences and opportunities. For Mannheim (1952), as explained in Chapter Two, such shared exposure may lead each cohort to be ideologically distinctive from another, creating 'social generations'.

The importance of cohort as an element in the ageing process has been indicated throughout this book. For example, each of the chapters on the main life course stages includes a section where historical comparisons are drawn. Whenever historical evidence on a particular life course stage is presented, it is essentially the experiences of earlier *cohorts* that is being considered. More specific references to cohort processes have also featured in previous chapters. For example, in Chapter Four, direct comparisons were drawn between the experiences of two broad cohorts of young people, namely those who were young in the 1950s and 1960s and those who were young in the 1980s and 1990s.

In Chapter Five, the redefinition of the middle years of life as the 'new middle age' was argued to be, in part, a consequence of the young people of the 1950s and 1960s bringing the cultural tastes and values of their youth with them as they enter middle age. Cohort processes were also mentioned in relation to the experiences of currently elderly women (Chapter Six). It was argued, furthermore, that future cohorts of elderly women are likely to enter old age with a contrasting set of material and cultural resources. Finally, in the previous chapter, the challenges brought about by an ageing population were explained, in part, as a consequence of variations in the size of birth cohorts. Such fluctuations mean that future cohorts of elderly people may be reliant on support provided for them by a relatively small cohort of adults of working age. In these various ways, then, cohort processes have been an important theme running throughout this book. Within this chapter, cohort processes become the main focus of concern. They are argued to 'set the framework for individuals' existence and development, affecting their life chances, their view of the world, their aspirations and their prospects' (Rosow 1978: 69). To this end, evidence on the importance of cohort membership in terms of the ways in which it acts to shape opportunities and experiences of individuals is reviewed. The existence of cohorts with distinctive political and cultural identities is also considered.

Fortunes of Birth

Demographic data discussed in detail elsewhere in this book have shown the extent to which the historical period into which someone happens to have been born directly affects their life chances. The likelihood of individuals surviving infancy, their propensity to marry, their age at marriage, the number of children, the likelihood of living long enough to see grandchildren born and grow up, and age at death, can all be predicted according to the period in history through which they lived (Anderson 1985). Of course, more information than just date of birth is required to predict with greater accuracy the precise range of experiences and opportunities likely to have been open to them, but knowing which cohort someone belongs to can help paint a picture of the broad historical context of their lives. For example, a man born in 1895 would have been 20 in 1915 and thus likely to have been a soldier in the First World War. A young woman entering the labour market at age 14 in 1920 is likely to have given up work on her marriage, since a

Figure 8.1
Opportunities
vary by cohort
membership

Source: Posy
Simmonds.
Reproduced
with permission
from the artist.

136

marriage bar (for women) was in operation in many occupations until at least the beginning of the Second World War. During the war, the same woman might have been encouraged to rejoin the labour market, perhaps working in munitions factories. As Figure 8.1 depicts, different generations of the same family can experience greatly contrasting sets of experiences and opportunities, according to the point in history at which they were born.

When a person is born clearly acts to shape his or her life in a whole variety of ways. It is also the case that cohort *size* can be an important determinant of an individual's fate and fortune. We have already seen, in the previous chapter, how changes in the age structure in the future may mean that a small cohort of working age will have to contribute a significant proportion of their income in taxes to support a large cohort of dependent elderly people. An increase in the numbers of young people in the late 1970s and early 1980s was a contributory factor to the problems many experienced in making the transition from education to the labour market (Chapter Four). Specific analyses have been made of the impact cohort size can have on the economic opportunities of its members (for example, Ermisch 1988; Wright 1991). Findings point to the tendency for members of large cohorts to earn less (at least, during the early part of their working lives) as a direct consequence of 'cohort crowding', whereby there is increased competition for places in the occupational structure. As with discussions of the dependency ratio, though, we need to be wary of demographic determinism. The magnitude of the problems caused by cohort crowding, as Bloom *et al.* (1987) point out, is influenced by factors other than demographic ones, especially the prevailing economic conditions and social policy responses. Johnson and Falkingham (1992) make the point that, although evidence is patchy, changes in the age structure of the population have the *potential* to alter patterns of consumption of goods and services (including housing), savings and investment, and innovation, as well as patterns of employment. Coleman and Salt (1992), in a similar vein, note that the population of working age accounts for much of the productive capacities of the economy and is also a paramount consumer group. They argue that the 'baby boomers', who currently make up an important element of the population of working age, are a vital market for private sector goods and services. As they grow older, it is likely that there will be an expansion in demand for goods and services characteristic of older age groups. Coleman and Salt note that marketing departments now pay great attention to likely shifts in demand arising from age-structure changes.

Cohort: Culture and Socio-Political Orientations

This section considers the existence of culturally distinctive cohorts and the influence of cohort on socio-political attitudes and orientations. Mannheim's theory of social generations, which elaborates the concept of cohort by arguing that location in historical time leads to ideological distinctiveness, is relevant to both of these areas of investigation. Briefly considered in Chapter Two, this theory will now be set out in greater detail.

Mannheim's essay on cohort processes is regarded as seminal because it firmly locates cohort within socio-historical contexts, and moreover, is part of a wider sociological theory of knowledge. For Mannheim, 'knowledge' (defined by him as a style of thought or world view) is seen as socially conditioned by its location in a socio-historical structure. While discussions in the sociology of knowledge have focused on class location (Abercrombie 1980), Mannheim also identifies cohort location as a key element in the social determination of knowledge. Cohort location, like class location, points to 'certain definite modes of behaviour, feeling and thought' (Mannheim 1952: 291). In the case of class location, an individual or group's position emerges from the existence of an economic and power structure within society. The structure from which cohort location emerges is the 'existence of biological rhythm in human existence—the factors of life and death, a limited span of life, and ageing' (Mannheim 1952: 290). Although recognizing the influence of biological factors, Mannheim stresses the overriding and ultimate importance of social factors, so that biology is seen to be embedded within social and historical processes. Mannheim is not, of course, implying that mere chronological contemporaneity produces a common consciousness: indeed his contention is that 'all people living at the same time do not necessarily share the same history' (Troll 1970: 201). Consequently, contemporaries may experience the same social and cultural phenomena or historical events differently.

For Mannheim, chronologically contemporaneous individuals (that is, all persons now alive) are stratified by the tendency for the formative experiences and early impressions of youth to 'coalesce into a natural view of the world' (Mannheim 1952: 298). Individuals carry this with them throughout the life span. People are thus crucially influenced by the socio-historical context that predominated in their youth, and in this way, social generations have distinctive historically determined world views. Mannheim is proposing that in order to share social generational location in a sociologically meaningful sense, individuals must be born within the same historical and cultural context and be exposed to particular experiences and events that occur during their formative adult years. This is the general level of social generational location identified by Mannheim. He also provides a more specific and sophisticated analysis of social generational location. First, he recognizes that geographical and cultural location will act to internally differentiate social generations, so that not every member will be exposed to exactly the same experiences. Secondly, he distinguishes between those social generational groupings who actually participate in the social and cultural events of their time and place and those who do not. Thirdly, he recognizes that within 'actual' social generations, there may arise differing and opposing *responses* to social and cultural events, in that there may develop opposing social generational 'units'.

Mannheim's discussion of social generations is integrally concerned with the issue of social change (Laufer and Bengtson 1974). Thus he maintains that the likelihood of a cohort developing a distinctive consciousness (of becoming a social generation) is dependent on the *tempo* of social change. In turn, social generations are regarded as a key element in the *production* of social change. The 'fresh contact' of new cohorts with the already existing cultural and social heritage always means a 'changed relationship of distance' and a 'novel approach in assimilating, using and developing the proffered material' (Mannheim 1952: 293). The progression of social change is made smoother by the presence of 'intermediary' (or buffer) social generations. The implication here is that social generations with the least difference in world views or styles of thought are always adjacent to one another, whilst those with the greatest difference are non-adjacent. In times of accelerated social change, however, when normality is disrupted, the 'new brooms' have even greater opportunity and access than the natural, gradual change-over, brought about by the ageing and eventual death of all members of a cohort, allows.

Culturally Distinctive Cohorts

It was the emergence of the distinctive youth cultures of the 1960s that led to a renewal of interest in the writings of Mannheim, amongst other theorists. We have already seen, in Chapter Four, how many commentators during the 1960s identified a 'rivalry' between young people and

139

adults and, in general, regarded youth as being at the vanguard of social change. In Britain, the youth culture of the 1960s had both political and cultural manifestations. Politically, it was characterized by the student protest movement, by campaigns and demonstrations against the Vietnam War and nuclear weapons, and by the activities of community action groups; in short, by activist politics and by radical, libertarian philosophies. Culturally, the youth culture of the 1960s amounted to a 'living' of their politics, through practising counter-cultural life-styles: communes, drug use, sexual liberation. Such life-styles were epitomized in the 'hippie culture'. The common theme of the cultural and political wings of the 'sixties generation' was the critique and rejection of the status quo: of established social institutions, conventions, values, and behaviours. Mannheim's theory can be applied to the phenomenon of the 1960s youth culture. In Mannheim's terms, the 'fresh contact' with the already existing social and cultural heritage by young people in the 1960s led to a 'novel approach' in assimilating, using, and developing it. The accelerated social changes of the post-war decades (see Chapter Four) gave the 'new broom' of youth the opportunity to engage in cultural innovation and contribute to social change. Mannheim's theory allows for the fact that not every young person in the 1960s was part of what might be called the 'actual sixties social generation': not every youthful person actively participated in the social and cultural events of the time. Mannheim's theory also allows for the existence of opposing 'social generational units', such as pro- and anti-Vietnam war campaigners.

The response to the politics and culture of 1960s youth on the part of the older cohort of 'moral guardians and the control culture' (Clarke *et al.* 1976) was to engage in moral panics about the crisis of authority and the dangers of permissiveness. As Clarke *et al.* (1976) describe it, the reaction of the authorities took the form of legal actions and trials, including arrests and the use of conspiracy charges, a clamp-down on drug use and on the publication of 'pornography'. Frith (1984) argues that the 1960s did contribute to social change in that the cultural legacy of the 1960s can be found in the women's movement, in the gay and animal liberation movements, in the squatters movement, and in the Green (ecology) movement. More generally, alternative cultures in contemporary Britain, such as the New Age Travellers, the rave scene, and drug use, can be argued to have their roots in the 1960s.

It is the 'sixties generation' that seems to represent the archetypal culturally distinctive cohort within modern British history. Certainly, there remains a high level of *public* awareness of the 1960s, so much so that the 'sixties generation' is a shorthand term to refer to liberalism, permissiveness, and a whole host of other associated characteristics. Undoubtedly, there has been a degree of both mythologizing and demonizing about the 1960s. As suggested above, Mannheim's theory of social generations can be used to interpret the 1960s phenomenon in a broad sense. However, there have been few systematic, detailed sociological studies of the causes, extent, nature, and legacy of the 1960s phenomenon in Britain. Much of what has been said remains at a very general level of conjecture. More research needs to be done on the 'sixties generation' before a full assessment of its sociological significance can be made. Studies influenced by Mannheim's theory have, though, been more frequent in America, where some evidence suggests that values and behaviours of the 'sixties generation' are retained by individuals as they age. A 'liberal orientation' has been found to endure beyond youth, persisting into adulthood and middle age. Similarly, a degree of 'freakiness', such as smoking marijuana and a toleration of unconventional life-styles, has been shown to be retained by some individuals who were part of the 1960s cohort. The authors of such studies suggest that the duration and persistence of such attitudes and behaviours will lead to social change in American culture in the future (see studies cited in Bengtson *et al.* 1974).

Cohort Influences on Socio-Political Attitudes and Orientations

Survey evidence shows the importance of age in predicting socio-political attitudes (see box overleaf), but as Abrams (1972: 109) puts it, such data 'only describe our problem'. Why is it that younger age groups demonstrate a tendency to hold more progressive attitudes than shown by older age groups?

The findings of age differences by the British Social Attitudes survey, shown in the box, were explained as a function of cohort processes. This is also the explanation favoured by one recent study which used Mannheim's theory in explanation of differences found in the accounts three generations of women gave about feminist issues, feminism, and the women's movement (Pilcher 1992). In order to illustrate how cohort processes are argued to influence socio-political orientations, this study will be referred to in some detail. A sample of three-generational families of women were asked for their opinions on a range of issues, including role reversal, the existence and extent of inequality and discrimination against women, abortion, and homosexuality. They were also asked about their knowledge of and opinion toward feminism and feminists. Mannheim's theory of social generations was used to analyse the women's responses. In the study of three generations of women's accounts of feminism, their dates of birth were used to determine their cohort location in historical time. The words and phrases (vocabularies) made use of by the women were located, or placed, within the context of their likely formative socio-historical experiences. Two broad groupings of vocabularies used by the women were identified. *Traditionalist* vocabularies conveyed an orientation to past cultural practices and a disdain of contemporary cultural practices. Examples of traditionalist vocabularies include speaking of 'a man's place' as a breadwinner and 'a woman's place' in the home, of denying that women *should* be equal to men, of being hostile to abortion and homosexuality. *Progressive* vocabularies conveyed an orientation to present cultural practices and a toleration and advocation of change, along with a disdain for past cultural practices. Examples of progressive vocabularies include approval of men engaging in housework and child care, approval of equal pay and equal opportunities for women, toleration of homosexuality, and support for a woman's right to abortion. It was found that the oldest generation of women (born *c*.1914) tended to make use of traditionalist vocabularies, whilst the youngest generation (born *c*.1965) tended to make use of progressive vocabularies. The middle generation (born *c*.1945) fell in between the greater traditionalism of the oldest generation and the greater progressiveness of the younger generation, a finding predicted by Mannheim's point about 'buffer' social generations. One striking example of the differences between the 'world views' of the three generations of women was in terms of their familiarity with the term 'feminism' itself. Women of the oldest generation were found to be almost completely unfamilliar with the term feminism. These women either did not know what feminism was at all, or they took it to mean 'feminine qualities', either in women (as in femininity) or in men (as in effeminacy). However, the women were familiar with the terms 'women's liberation' or 'women's lib'. In the case of the middle generation of women, feminism was something that most were familiar with. Only a handful said that it was something they had not heard of or could not say what it was. Several, though, did misinterpret feminism to mean femininity in women. Almost all of the youngest generation of women knew what feminism was and were able to provide appropriate descriptions or definitions of it. Such differences in the accounts given by the three generations of women were argued to be a consequence of the contrasting socio-historical contexts of their life courses (Pilcher 1992; 1994b). In other words, their membership of different cohorts, to paraphrase Rosow (1978), set the framework for their existence and has affected their view of the world.

Cohort processes can be identified as an important influence on people's socio-political orientations, in the ways outlined above. However, evidence cannot be regarded as conclusive. The empirical study of the formation, development, and retention of world views over the life course is made problematical by the complex entangling of two further 'time' elements, in addition to cohort or social generational experiences: those of ageing or individual biography and of historical or period events (see also Chapter Two). Consequently, researchers may emphasize any one, or a combination, of these three central influences. Stage in life course effects, as in 'rebellious youth' or 'conservative old age', may be invoked. Period effects (historical, political, or economic events or crises) may be seen to influence the world views of people of all ages and cohorts. Finally, explanations may centre around cohort effects, which arise from the importance of adolescent and early adulthood experiences within particular historical contexts for the formation of world views, which then persist over the life span. Empirically, it is difficult, if not impossible, to separate these three central influences (Alwin et al. 1991). 'People do not grow up and grow old in laboratories' (Riley 1984: 8); they do so within society and within history. This is the source of the complexity surrounding the investigation and interpretation of all age-related phenomena.

The authors of one major recent study (Alwin *et al.* 1991) favour the 'generational-persistence model' as a 'useful' summary of what is known about the formation and development of socio-political orientations over the life course. The 'generational-persistence model' (or more properly, the *cohort*-persistence model) has three components. First, the notion of a period of vulnerability to influence, occurring in late adolescence and early adulthood. Second, the notion that each new cohort experiences that time of life differently, and that there are unique residues within the individual because of those experiences. Third, the notion that, after some early period of influence and change, attitudes become crystallized and increasingly stable with age (Alwin *et al.* 1991: 264). Research evidence is particularly supportive of the first and third components of the model. The importance of late adolescence as a key period of socialization is widely accepted (for review, see Braungart 1984). Moreover, research has found that people of all ages tend to report historical events and changes that occurred in their youth as especially important or meaningful (Schuman and Scott 1989; Stewart and Healy 1989). Evidence also strongly supports the notion that, once formed, world views are retained over the life span (Braungart 1984). Whilst considerable evidence exists in support of the first and third components of the model, opinion as to the long-term effects of social generational or cohort experiences (the second component) is rather mixed. In reviews of available evidence, some conclude that there is a degree of support for long-term social generational effects (for example, Roberts and Lang 1985), albeit 'meagre' (Alwin *et al.* 1991). Others argue that little systematic evidence exists for the lasting effects of social generational experiences (for example, Schuman and Reiger 1992). Still others find that social generational differences may vary as a function of particular issues (for example, Glass *et al.* 1986; Kalish and Johnson 1972; Sears 1983). Alwin *et al.* (1991) reach the conclusion that evidence (including their own) supports the 'generational-persistence model'. However, they argue that the model may give too much emphasis to cohort processes and neglect other variables. They also suggest that the model may give too much emphasis to the stability of orientations over an individual's life course, in the face of evidence which shows that changes do occur over time.

This chapter has concentrated on the importance of cohort membership. Evidence has been presented which shows that an individual's location in historical time, via the cohort to which they belong, can impact upon most aspects of their existence, from their longevity to their knowledge of what the term feminism means. Experiences and opportunities available to individuals have also been shown to be influenced by the size of the cohort to which an individual belongs. It should also be clear from this discussion of the importance of cohort that, although life courses are affected by location in historical time and the character of the cohort to which people belong, the changed experiences of individuals and cohorts also leads to large scale changes in social and cultural structures (Hess 1988). For example, societal institutions have had to respond to 'cohort crowding' and have had to address, as they will in the future, the needs of an ageing population. The 'sixties generation' can be argued to have brought about a degree of social and cultural change across society. As Abrams (1982) explains, individuals are constructed historically by society, but in turn, society is a process constructed historically by individuals. The relationship is a reciprocal, dialectical one, whereby individuals both constitute historical configurations and are constituted historically by them.

Further Reading

Johnson and Falkingham (1992) is a good starting-point for further references on the impact of demographic restructuring on the macroeconomy. An extract from Mannheim's essay on social generations can be found in Jenks (1982). The contributions edited by Crick and Robson (1970) provide a flavourful account of the politics of the 1960s youth culture.

Chapter Nine

From Here to Post-modernity?

This book has drawn together a range of evidence which shows the important role age plays in shaping experiences and relationships and in structuring access to power, resources, and citizenship rights within modern Britain. This concluding chapter does not attempt to summarize the wealth of evidence about the social significance of age, generation, and cohort in modern Britain. Instead, the emphasis is on reviewing reasons why age has become an increasingly important area of sociological inquiry.

The life course perspective has been emphasized throughout this book as a useful way of thinking sociologically about age. It allows us to understand the role social, cultural, economic, and political factors play in shaping the social significance of age, including the ways in which life courses are subject to differentiation by structures of inequality based on class, gender, and ethnicity. Thinking about the life course as a social institution linked with other social institutions in society sensitizes us to the effects social changes in these institutions have upon the shape of the life course, the sequencing and duration of its constituent stages, and the transitions that individuals make between them. Historical evidence drawn upon throughout this book has shown that what we recognize as the modern life course, and the especial characteristics of each of its stages, is a relatively recent development. It is one linked closely to the socio-economic transformations brought about by industrialization, which changed Britain from a pre-modern to a modern society. The form of the life course and the characteristics of each life course stage described in this book did not really come into being until the early decades of the twentieth century and did not become fully established until the middle of this century. The modern forms of the life course stages childhood and youth have emerged via a process of their progressive exclusion from the labour market and their increasing containment within the education system. These processes have been fundamentally important in constructing childhood and youth as stages of the life course characterized by dependency and relative powerlessness. The modern form of the old age stage of the life course similarly emerged via a process of exclusion from the labour market and containment within the institution of retirement. These processes have in turn led old age to be constructed as a period of dependency and relative powerlessness. Adulthood, as the materially and ideologically dominant stage of the life course, emerged largely as a result of the exclusion of the earlier and later life course stages, so that it was adulthood that came to be equated with full personhood and independence, via participation in the labour market. These changes brought about by processes linked to industrialization have transformed the importance of age. Whilst in pre-modern society, age had limited importance in terms of access to power, resources, and citizenship rights, in modern society, as evidence presented through-out this book has shown, age is a fundamentally important social division.

The form and characteristics of the modern British life course itself can, then, be argued to be the product of the interrelations of societal institutions as they have developed under conditions of modernity. The population structure of contemporary British society can also be explained in terms of the conditions of modernity. The ageing of the population is largely a consequence of a decline in fertility, but is also influenced by increasing longevity. The greater certainties of modern society (full employment, state welfare provision, rising standards of living) have had long-term consequences for the shape of the popula-tion and so for the duration of overlaps between generations and cohorts. Anderson (1985) describes the modern British life course as having the quality of 'orderliness'. Most people can now expect to progress through childhood, youth, adulthood, and old age, and as they do so, to move through a number of dependent and independent statuses, enter into a range of relationships, and engage with a variety of different societal institutions.

Yet, it is increasingly being argued that there are emerging trends toward a 'disorder of things modern' (Smart 1990). The uncertainty and disorder is illustrated by deindustrialization, whereby the industrial sector has declined and the service sector has grown. Rather than full employment and strong trades unions, the conditions of the labour market have been transformed. Flexible employment patterns are encouraged and the strength of organized labour has been reduced. Rather than comprehensive, extensive public sector provision, there has been a stress on reducing the public sector, including the scope of the welfare state. People's health and welfare needs are argued to be better met by private, individual provision, rather than by state. The 'disorder of things modern' is also reflected in the decline of traditional family forms, with family life increasingly characterized by diversity. Fewer people are marrying and are having fewer children, more people are cohabiting and having children outside marriage, and more people are living alone. In the cultural sphere, science and religion have lost their hegemonic status and have become less relevant as sources of meaning for people in their everyday lives, whilst the mass media has assumed a high degree of cultural significance. The gradual erosion of long-standing frames of reference, including class, family, community, and religion, means that people are less secure in their personal and collective identities (Strinati 1992). Consequently, people are increasingly concerned with issues of self-identity, expressed through a concern with image and fashion and the presentation of self through the appearance of the body. In short, the argument has been proposed that, as Giddens (1991) describes it, in 'high modernity' or in the 'post-traditional social universe', or as others have described it, in 'post-modernity', there have been important changes in many of the fundamental aspects of social life.

At the beginning of this book, it was argued that age is a relatively neglected area of sociological inquiry. The evidence presented in this book is testimony to the increasing attention being paid to its social significance. The fact that sociologists have become increasingly interested in age and age relationships can be argued to be a consequence of the newly emerging set of socio-economic and cultural transformations, which have been summarized as a 'disorder of things modern' (Smart 1990). Often, it is only when things which were previously believed to be largely natural begin to undergo change that we fully recognize their socially constructed nature. Increased sociological interest in age can, then, be understood in the context of three related developments within society. First, in the context of a range of socio-economic and cultural changes which have impacted upon the life course. Second, in the context of demographic changes, especially the ageing of the population, which has raised issues about relationships between generations, between people at different stages of the life course, and between different cohorts. Third, in the context of the development of medical techniques which introduce the possibility of altering physiological ageing processes. The impact of these developments on the social significance of age is outlined below.

Various chapters within this book have described changes to education and the labour market, to social policy, to family formation and kinship relationships, all of which have implications for the timing and sequencing of transitions that individuals make between stages of the life course. Such changes have been shown to have consequences for individuals, their families, and for society at large. Some theorists have argued that, in effect, the life course is becoming deinstitutionalized and destandardized, that age-based transitions and norms, forms, and standards of behaviour, which previously were fairly strictly defined, regulated, and orderly, are becoming less fixed, less constraining, less orderly, and less subject to differentiation by class, gender, and ethnicity. What evidence is there in support of these claims? As shown in Chapter Three, arguments have been made to the effect that modern childhood is losing its distinctive characteristics, that children are becoming more like adults. Recent changes in the transition to adulthood experienced by modern youth (Chapter Four) are also cited as evidence of the destandardization of the life course. Norms and values associated with the middle years of life are also argued to have undergone change, in part linked to changes in 'workending' (Chapter Five). Education is argued to have become less age-specific, with rising numbers of mature students entering the further and higher education system. The life course of families has undergone fragmentation arising from trends in marriage, divorce, and single parenthood, so that families themselves are reconstituted and 'family time' is rather more disorderly. Changes in the age at family formation and the clustering of childrearing in the early part of the life course, combined with increasing longevity, now mean that grandparenthood can now be the experience of a vast age range of persons, from, say, age 35 to 105. Increased longevity has also led to the emergence of new stages of the life course: the 'very very elderly' or the 'oldest old'. Changing employment patterns of women mean that more and more women are having their first babies later in life, which may have implications for the duration and nature of relationships between the generations in future. An important area of change which has impacted on the social significance of age is developments in medical or pseudo-medical technologies. Techniques have increasingly become available which enable people to delay, alter, or even overcome some of the physiological aspects of ageing. Examples here would be cosmetic surgery, including face lifts, and medical procedures which allow post-menopausal women to have children. Such technological developments can mean that what were understood as natural processes of ageing are increasingly subject to alterations and an element of human control. Some analysts of 'the disorder of things modern' argue that one consequence of the search for meaning and values that accompanies uncertainty is a rise in the symbolic value of the body as a bearer of status. Various chapters within this book have shown the importance of the 'exterior territories' (Mellor and Shilling 1993) of the body as a signifier of social status throughout the life course.

The changes reviewed above certainly suggest that things are no longer what they have more recently been in terms of the structuring of life course stages and the norms and standards of behaviour associated with life course stages. The 'orderliness' of the life course characteristic of the middle decades of the twentieth century is now rather less orderly. The concept of the life course is, though, flexible enough to continue to accommodate the changes occurring in the socio-economic and cultural conditions of contemporary British society. Moreover, the balance of the evidence in this book points to the continuing importance of age-based social divisions (mediated by class, gender, and ethnicity) that are a consequence of meanings attached to physiological ageing processes, the construction of life course stages, and the difference in opportunities and identities resulting from cohort membership.

References

ABERCROMBIE, N. (1980), *Class, Structure and Knowledge*, Oxford: Basil Blackwell.
—— *et al.* (1994), *Contemporary British Society*, 2nd edn., Cambridge: Polity.
ABRAMS, M. (1959), *The Teenage Consumer*, London: London Press Exchange Papers No. 5.
ABRAMS, P. (1972), 'Age and Generation' in P. Barker (ed.), *A Sociological Portrait*, Harmondsworth: Penguin.
—— (1982), *Historical Sociology*, Somerset: Open Books.
AIREY, C., and BROOK, L. (1986), 'Interim Report: Social and Moral Issues', in R. Jowell, S. Witherspoon, and L. Brook (eds.), *British Social Attitudes*, Aldershot: Gower.
ALANEN, L. (1988), 'Rethinking Childhood', *Acta Sociologica*, 31: 53–67.
ALLATT, P., and KEIL, T. (1987), 'Introduction', in P. Allatt *et al.* (eds.), *Women and the Life Cycle*, London: Macmillan.
—— *et al.* (1987) (eds.), *Women and the Life Cycle*, London: Macmillan.
ALWIN, D., COHEN, R., and NEWCOMB, T. (1991), *Political Attitudes over the Life Span: The Bennington Women after Fifty Years*, Madison, Wis.: University of Wisconsin Press.
ANDERSON, M. (1985), 'The Emergence of the Modern Life Cycle in Britain', *Social History*, 10: 69–87.
ARBER, S., and GINN, J. (1991), *Gender and Later Life*, London: Sage.
ARCHARD, D. (1993), *Children: Rights and Childhood*, London: Routledge.
ARIES, P. (1962), *Centuries of Childhood*, London: Jonathan Cape.
ASHTON, D., MAGUIRE, D., and GARLAND, V. (1982), *Youth in the Labour Market*, Department of Employment Research Paper No. 34, London: HMSO.
BABAD, E., BIRNBAUM, M., and BENNE, K. (1983), *The Social Self: Group Influences on Personal Identity*, London: Sage.
BALDING, J. (1987), *Young People in 1986*, Exeter: Health Education Authority.
BELLABY, P. (1987), 'The Perpetuation of a Folk Model of the Life Cycle and Kinship in a Pottery Factory', in A. Bryman *et al.* (eds.), *Rethinking the Life Cycle*, London: Macmillan.
BENEDICT, R. (1955), 'Continuities and Discontinuities in Cultural Conditioning', in M. Mead and M. Wolfenstein (eds.), *Childhood in Contemporary Cultures*, Chicago: University of Chicago Press.
BENGTSON, V., FURLONG, M., and LAUFER, R. (1974), 'Time, Aging and the Continuity of Social Structure: Themes and Issues in Generational Analysis', *Journal of Social Issues*, 30: 1–30.
BERNARD, M., and MEADE, K. (1993*a*), 'Perspectives on the Lives of Older Women', in M. Bernard and K. Meade (eds.), *Women Come of Age*, London: Edward Arnold.

References

BERNARD, M., and MEADE, K. (1993*b*), 'A Third Age Lifestyle for Older Women?', in M. Bernard and K. Meade (eds.), *Women Come of Age*, London: Edward Arnold.

BLAKEMORE, K. (1989), 'Does Age Matter? The Case of Old Age in Ethnic Minority Groups' in B. Bytheway *et al.* (eds.), *Becoming and Being Old*, London: Sage.

—— and BONEHAM, M. (1994), *Age, Race and Ethnicity*, Milton Keynes: Open University Press.

BLOOM, D., FREEMAN, R., and KORENMAN, S. (1987), 'The Labour Market Consequences of Generational Crowding', *European Journal of Population*, 3: 131–76.

BOND, J., BRIGGS, R., and COLEMAN, P. (1990), 'The Study of Ageing', in J. Bond and P. Coleman (eds.), *Ageing in Society*, London: Sage.

BOYDEN, J. (1990), 'Childhood and the Policy Makers: A Comparative Perspective on the Globalization of Childhood', in A. James and A. Prout (eds.), *Constructing and Reconstructing Childhood*, London: Falmer.

BRAKE, M. (1980), *The Sociology of Youth Culture and Youth Subcultures*, London: RKP.

—— (1985), *Comparative Youth Culture*, London: RKP.

BRANNEN, J., DODD, K., OAKLEY, A., and STOREY, P. (1994), *Young People, Health and Family Life*, Milton Keynes: Open University Press.

—— and WILSON, G. (1987) (eds.), *Give and Take in Families*, London: Allen and Unwin.

BRAUNGART, M. (1984), 'Aging and Politics', *Journal of Military and Political Sociology*, 12: 79–98.

BROOKES-GUNN, J., and KIRSCH, B. (1984), 'Life Events and the Boundaries of Midlife for Women', in G. Baruch and J. Brookes-Gunn (eds.), *Women in Midlife*, New York: Plenum Press.

BROWN, P. (1990), 'Schooling and Economic Life in the United Kingdom', in L. Chisholm *et al.* (eds.), *Childhood, Youth and Social Change: A Comparative Perspective*, London: Falmer.

BRYMAN, A. *et al.* (1987) (eds.), *Rethinking the Life Cycle*, London: Macmillan.

CARTER, M. (1962), *Home, School and Work*, Oxford: Permagon Press.

Central Statistical Office (1994*a*), *Social Trends 24*, London: HMSO.

—— (1994*b*), *Family Spending: A Report on the 1993 Family Expenditure Survey*, London: HMSO.

Children's Rights Development Unit (1993), *The Rights of the Child: A Guide to the UN Convention*, London: Department of Health.

CHISHOLM, L. (1990), 'A Sharper Lens or a New Camera? Youth Research, Young People and Social Change in Britain', in L. Chisholm *et al.* (eds.), *Childhood, Youth and Social Change: A Comparative Perspective*, London: Falmer.

—— *et al.* (1990), 'Childhood and Youth Studies in the United Kingdom and West Germany: An Introduction', in L. Chisholm *et al.* (eds.), *Childhood, Youth and Social Change: A Comparative Perspective*, London: Falmer.

—— BUCHNER, P., KRUGER, H., and BROWN, P. (1990) (eds.), *Childhood, Youth and Social Change: A Comparative Perspective*, London: Falmer.

CLARKE, J., HALL, S., JEFFERSON, T., and ROBERTS, B. (1976), 'Subcultures, Cultures and Class: A Theoretical Overview', in S. Hall and T. Jefferson (eds.), *Resistance through Rituals*, London: Hutchinson.

COFFIELD, F. (1987), 'From the Celebration to the Marginalization of Youth', in G. Cohen (ed.), *Social Change and the Life Course*, London: Tavistock.

COLE, T. (1989), 'Generational Equity in America: A Cultural Historian's Perspective', *Social Science and Medicine*, 29: 377–83.

COLEMAN, D. (1988), 'Population', in A. Halsey (ed.), *British Social Trends Since 1900*, London: Macmillan.

—— and SALT, J. (1992), *The British Population: Patterns, Trends and Processes*, Oxford: Oxford University Press.

COTTERILL, P. (1992), ' "But for Freedom, You See, not to Be a Baby-minder": Women's Attitudes toward Grandmother Care', *Sociology*, 26: 603–18.

COWGILL, D., and HOLMES, L. (1972) (eds.), *Aging and Modernization*, New York: Appleton.

CRAIG, T. (1993), 'The late late learning show', *Guardian*, 11 May.

CRICK, B., and ROBSON, W. (1970) (eds.), *Protest and Discontent*, Harmondsworth: Penguin.

Critical Social Policy (1986–7), No. 18, Winter.

CUMMING, E., and HENRY, W. (1961), *Growing Old: The Process of Disengagement*, New York: Basic Books.

Department of Social Security (1994), *Households below Average Income*, London: HMSO.

DOWD, J. (1986), 'The Old Person as Stranger', in V. Marshall (ed.), *The Social Psychology of Aging*, London: Sage.

EISENSTADT, S. N. (1956), *From Generation to Generation*, London: Routledge and Kegan Paul.

ENNEW, J. (1986), *The Sexual Exploitation of Children*, Cambridge: Polity.

ERMISCH, J. (1988), 'Fortunes of Birth: The Impact of Generation Size on the Relative Earnings of Young Men', *Scottish Journal of Political Economy*, 35: 266–82.

ESLER, A. (1984), ' "The Truest Community": Social Generations as Collective Mentalities', *Journal of Political and Military Sociology*, 12: 99–112.

ESTES, C. (1986), 'The Politics of Aging in America', *Ageing and Society*, 6: 121–34.

FALKINGHAM, J. (1989), 'Dependency and Ageing in Britain: A Re-examination of the Evidence', *Journal of Social Policy*, 18: 211–33.

FEATHERSTONE, M., and HEPWORTH, M. (1989), 'Ageing and Old Age: Reflections on the Postmodern Life Course', in B. Bytheway *et al.* (eds.), *Becoming and Being Old*, London: Sage.

—— —— (1990), 'Images of Ageing', in J. Bond and P. Coleman (eds.), *Ageing in Society*, London: Sage.

FENNELL, G., PHILLIPSON, C., and EVERS, E. (1988), *The Sociology of Old Age*, Milton Keynes: Open University Press.

FERRI, E. (1993) (ed.), *Life at 33: The Fifth Follow-up of the National Child Development Study*, London: National Children's Bureau.

References

FIELD, M., and FIELD, M. (1980), *Transitions: Four Rituals in Eight Cultures*, New York: W. W. Norton.

FINCH, J. (1986), 'Age' in R. Burgess (ed.), *Key Variables in Social Investigation*, London: RKP.

—— (1987), 'Family Obligations and the Life Course', in A. Bryman *et al.* (eds.), *Rethinking the Life Cycle*, London: Macmillan.

—— (1989), *Family Obligations and Social Change*, Cambridge: Polity.

—— and MASON, J. (1993), *Negotiating Family Responsibilities*, London: Routledge.

FIRESTONE, S. (1979), 'Down with Childhood', in M. Hoyles (ed.), *Changing Childhood*, London: Writers and Readers Co-operative.

FIRTH, R. (1970), 'Education in Tikopia', in J. Middleton (ed.), *From Child to Adult*, Austin: University of Texas Press.

FONER, N. (1984), 'Age and Social Change', in D. Kertzer and J. Keith (eds.), *Age and Anthropological Theory*, London: Cornell University Press.

FORTES, M. (1984), 'Age, Generation and Social Structure', in D. Kertzer and J. Keith (eds.), *Age and Anthropological Theory*, London: Cornell University Press.

FRITH, S. (1984), *The Sociology of Youth*, Lancashire: Causeway.

FYFE, A. (1989), *Child Labour*, Cambridge: Polity.

GIDDENS, A. (1991), *Modernity and Self Identity*, Cambridge: Polity.

GILLIS, J. (1974), *Youth and History*, New York: Academic Press.

GINN, J., and ARBER, S. (1992), 'Gender and Resources in Later Life', *Sociology Review*, 2 (2): 6–10.

GITTINS, D. (1993), *The Family in Question: Changing Households and Familiar Ideologies*, 2nd edn., London: Macmillan.

GLASS, J., BENGTSON, V., and CHORN DUNHAM, C. (1986), 'Attitude Similarity in Three Generation Families: Socialization, Status Inheritance or Reciprocal Influence', *American Sociological Review*, 51: 685–98.

GLENN, N. (1977), *Cohort Analysis*, London: Sage.

GRAUBARD, S. (1978), 'Preface', in E. Erikson (ed.), *Adulthood*, New York: W. W. Norton.

GREER, G. (1991), *The Change: Women, Ageing and the Menopause*, London: Hamish Hamilton.

GRIFFIN, C. (1985), *Typical Girls?*, London: Routledge.

—— (1987), 'Broken Transitions: From School to the Scrap Heap', in P. Allatt *et al.* (eds.), *Women and the Life Cycle*, London: Macmillan.

GROVES, D. (1993), 'Work, Poverty and Older Women', in M. Bernard and K. Meade (eds.), *Women Come of Age*, London: Edward Arnold.

HAKIM, C. (1987), *Research Design*, London: Allen and Unwin.

HARDING, S. (1988), 'Trends in Permissiveness', in R. Jowell, S. Witherspoon, and L. Brook (eds.), *British Social Attitudes*, Aldershot: Gower.

HAREVEN, T. (1978), 'The Last Stage: Historical Adulthood and Old Age', in E. Erikson (ed.), *Adulthood*, New York: W. W. Norton.

—— (1982*a*), 'Preface', in T. Hareven and K. Adams (eds.), *Ageing and Life Course Transitions*, London: Tavistock.

—— (1982*b*), *Family Time and Industrial Time*, Cambridge: Cambridge University Press.

HARPER, S., and THANE, P. (1989), 'The Consolidation of "Old Age" as a Phase of Life, 1945–65', in M. Jeffrys (ed.), *Growing Old in the Twentieth Century*, London: Routledge.

HARRIS, C. (1987), 'The Individual and Society: A Processual Approach', in A. Bryman *et al.* (eds.), *Rethinking the Life Cycle*, London: Macmillan.

HENDRICK, H. (1990), 'Constructions and Reconstructions of British Childhood: An Interpretative Survey, 1800 to the Present', in A. James and A. Prout (eds.), *Constructing and Reconstructing Childhood*, London: Falmer.

HENDRICKS, J., and HENDRICKS, C. (1979), 'Ageism and Common Stereotypes', in V. Carver and P. Liddiard (eds.), *An Ageing Population*, New York: Holmes and Meier.

HEPWORTH, M. (1987), 'The Midlife Phase', in G. Cohen (ed.), *Social Change and the Life Course*, London: Tavistock.

HESS, B. (1988), 'Social Structures and Human Lives: A Sociological Theme' in M. White Riley (ed.), *Social Structures and Human Lives*, Newbury Park: Sage.

HEWITT, R. (1990), 'Youth, Race and Language in Contemporary Britain: Deconstructing Ethnicity?', in L. Chisholm *et al.* (eds.), *Childhood, Youth and Social Change: A Comparative Perspective*, London: Falmer.

HILLMAN, M. (1993), 'One False Move: An Overview of the Findings and Issues They Raise', in M. Hillman (ed.), *Children, Transport and the Quality of Life*, London: Policy Studies Institute.

—— ADAMS, J., and WHITELEGG, J. (1991), *One False Move . . . A Study of Children's Independent Mobility*, London: Policy Studies Institute.

HOCKEY, J., and JAMES, A. (1993), *Growing up and Growing Old: Ageing and Dependency in the Life Course*, London: Sage.

HOLMES, L. (1974), *Somoan Village*, New York: Holt, Rinehart and Winston.

HOLT, J. (1974), *Escape from Childhood*, Harmondsworth: Penguin.

HOOD-WILLIAMS, J. (1990), 'Patriarchy for Children: On the Stability of Power Relations in Children's Lives', in L. Chisholm *et al.* (eds.), *Childhood, Youth and Social Change: A Comparative Perspective*, London: Falmer.

HOYLES, M. (1979) (ed.), *Changing Childhood*, London: Writers and Readers Co-operative.

HUGMAN, R. (1994), *Ageing and the Care of Older People in Europe*, London: Macmillan.

HUTSON, S., and JENKINS, R. (1989), *Taking the Strain: Families, Unemployment and the Transition to Adulthood*, Milton Keynes: Open University Press.

HUTTON, S. (1991), 'The Effects of Unemployment on the Early Years of Adult Life', *Youth and Policy*, No. 34: 18–25.

IKELS, C., *et al.* (1992), 'Perceptions of the Adult Life Course: A Cross Cultural Analysis', *Ageing and Society*, 12: 49–84.

IRWIN, S. (1990), 'Transitions in the Youth Debate: A Critique', in H. Corr and L. Jamieson (eds.), *Politics of Everyday Life*, London: Macmillan.

155

References

ITZIN, C. (1984), 'The Double Jeopardy of Ageism and Sexism: Media Images of Women', in D. Bromley (ed.), *Gerontology: Social and Behavioural Perspectives*, London: Croom Helm.

JACKSON, S. (1982), *Childhood and Sexuality*, Oxford: Basil Blackwell.

JAMES, A. (1986), 'Learning to Belong: The Boundaries of Adolescence', in A. Cohen (ed.), *Symbolising Boundaries: Identity and Diversity in British Cultures*, Manchester: Manchester University Press.

—— and PROUT, A. (1990) (eds.), *Constructing and Reconstructing Childhood: Contemporary Issues in the Sociological Study of Childhood*, London: Falmer.

JENKS, C. (1982) (ed.), *The Sociology of Childhood: Essential Readings*, London: Batsford.

JOHNSON, P. (1989), 'The Structured Dependency of the Elderly: A Critical Note', in M. Jeffrys (ed.), *Growing Old in the Twentieth Century*, London: Routledge.

—— and FALKINGHAM, J. (1992), *Ageing and Economic Welfare*, London: Sage.

JONES, G., and WALLACE, C. (1992), *Youth, Family and Citizenship*, Milton Keynes: Open University Press.

JORDAN, W. (1978), 'Searching for Adulthood in America', in E. Erikson (ed.), *Adulthood*, New York: W. W. Norton.

JURY, L., and DYER, C. (1994), 'Right to smack ruling sparks child care row', *Guardian*, 17 Mar.

KAGAN, D. (1980), 'Activity and Aging in a Columbian Peasant Village', in C. Fry (ed.), *Aging in Culture and Society*, New York: Praeger.

KALISH, R., and JOHNSON, A. (1972), 'Value Similarities and Differences in Three Generations of Women', *Journal of Marriage and the Family*, 34: 49–54.

KATCHADOURIAN, H. (1978), 'Medical Perspectives on Adulthood', in E. Erikson (ed.), *Adulthood*, New York: W. W. Norton.

KATZ, C. (1993), 'Growing Girls/Closing Circles: Limits on the Spaces of Knowing in Rural Sudan and U.S. Cities', in C. Katz and V. Monk (eds.), *Full Circles: Geographies of Women over the Life Course*, London: Routledge.

KERCKHOFF, A. (1990), *Getting Started: Transition to Adulthood in Great Britain*, San Francisco: Westview Press.

KIERNAN, K., and WICKS, M. (1990), *Family Change and Future Policy*, York: Joseph Rowntree Memorial Trust.

KOHLI, M. (1986), 'The World We Have Lost: A Historical Review of the Life Course', in V. Marshall (ed.), *The Social Psychology of Aging*, London: Sage.

—— (1988), 'Ageing as a Challenge for Sociological Theory', *Ageing and Society*, 8: 367–94.

LACZKO, F. (1989), 'Between Work and Retirement: Becoming "Old" in the 1980s', in B. Bytheway *et al.* (eds.), *Becoming and Being Old*, London: Sage.

LANGLEY, M. (1979), *The Nandi of Kenya: Life Crisis Rituals in a Period of Change*, London: Hurst and Co.

LASLETT, P. (1989), *A Fresh Map of Life: The Emergence of the Third Age*, London: Weidenfeld and Nicolson.

—— and FISHKIN, J. (1992), 'Introduction: Processional Justice', in P. Laslett and J. Fishkin (eds.), *Justice between Age Groups and Generations*, New Haven, Conn.: Yale University Press.

——— ——— (1992) (eds.), *Justice between Age Groups and Generations*, New Haven, Conn.: Yale University Press.

LAUFER, R., and BENGTSON, V. (1974), 'Generations, Aging and Social Stratification: On the Development of Generational Units', *Journal of Social Issues*, 30: 181–205.

LEE, D., and NEWBY, H. (1983), *The Problem of Sociology*, London: Hutchinson.

MACLEOD, P. (1994), 'Patten plans tougher truancy measures', *Guardian*, 9 Feb.

MACNICOL, J., and BLAIKIE, A. (1989), 'The Politics of Retirement, 1908–1948', in M. Jeffrys (ed.), *Growing Old in the Twentieth Century*, London: Routledge.

McROBBIE, A., and GARBER, J. (1976), 'Girls and Subcultures', in S. Hall and T. Jefferson (eds.), *Resistance through Rituals*, London: Hutchinson.

——— and NAVA, M. (1984) (eds.), *Gender and Generation*, London: Macmillan.

MAIN, B. (1988), 'The Lifetime Attachment of Women to the Labour Market', in A. Hunt (ed.), *Women and Paid Work*, London: Macmillan.

MAIZELS, J. (1970), *Adolescent Needs and the Transition from School to Work*, London: Althone Press.

MANNHEIM, K. (1952), 'The Problem of Generations', in K. Mannheim, *Essays on the Sociology of Knowledge*, London: RKP.

MELLOR, P., and SHILLING, C. (1993), 'Modernity, Self-identity and Sequestration of Death', *Sociology*, 27: 411–31.

MILLS, C. WRIGHT (1970), *The Sociological Imagination*, Harmondsworth: Penguin.

MILNE, K. (1994), 'Glad to be Grey', *New Statesman and Society*, 19 Aug.

MONK, J., and KATZ, C. (1993), 'When in the World are Women?', in C. Katz and J. Monk (eds.), *Full Circles: Geographies of Women over the Life Course*, London: Routledge.

MURDOCK, G., and McCRON, R. (1976), 'Consciousness of Class and Consciousness of Generation', in S. Hall and T. Jefferson (eds.), *Resistance through Rituals*, London: Hutchinson.

MURPHY, M. (1987), 'Measuring the Family Life Cycle: Concepts, Data and Methods', in A. Bryman *et al.* (eds.), *Rethinking the Life Cycle*, London: Macmillan.

NASH, L. (1978), 'Greek Origins of Generational Thought', *Daedalus*, 107: 1–22.

NEWSON, J., and NEWSON, E. (1976), *Seven Years Old in the Home Environment*, London: George Allen and Unwin.

O'CONNOR, P. (1991), 'Women's Confidants outside Marriage: Shared or Competing Sources of Intimacy?', *Sociology*, 25: 241–54.

O'DONNELL, M. (1985), *Age and Generation*, London: Tavistock.

OPCS (1977), *Marriage and Divorce Statistics 1974*, London: HMSO.

——— (1980), *Labour Force Survey 1973, 1975 and 1977*, London: HMSO.

——— (1987), *Labour Force Survey 1985*, London: HMSO.

——— (1992), *Labour Force Survey 1990 and 1991*, London: HMSO.

——— (1993*a*), *Topic Monitor 1991 Census: Ethnic Group and Country of Birth, Great Britain*, London: Government Statistical Service.

——— (1993*b*), *Topic Monitor 1991 Census: Sex, Age and Marital Status, Great Britain*, London: Government Statistical Service.

References

OPCS (1993c), *Topic Monitor 1991 Census: Persons Aged 60 and Over, Great Britain*, London: Government Statistical Service.

—— (1994a), *OPCS Monitor: National Population Projections, 1992 Based*, London: HMSO.

—— (1994b), *General Household Survey 1992*, London: HMSO.

—— (1994c), *General Household Survey: People Aged 65 and Over*, London: HMSO.

—— (1994d), *Day Care Services for Children*, London: HMSO.

OPIE, I. (1993), *The People in the Playground*, Oxford: Oxford University Press.

PARK, A. (1994), *England and Wales Youth Cohort Study, Cohort IV: Young People Aged 18–19 Years Old in 1991. Report on Sweep 3. Youth Cohort Report No. 29*, London: Employment Department.

PARSONS, T. (1954a), 'Age and Sex in the Social Structure of the United States', in T. Parsons, *Essays in Sociological Theory*, Glencoe: The Free Press.

—— (1954b), 'The Kinship System of the Contemporary United States', in T. Parsons, *Essays in Sociological Theory*, Glencoe: The Free Press.

PELLING, M., and SMITH, R. (1991), 'Introduction', in M. Pelling and R. Smith (eds.), *Life, Death and the Elderly: Historical Perspectives*, London: Routledge.

PHILLIPSON, C. (1982), *Capitalism and the Construction of Old Age*, London: Macmillan.

PILCHER, J. (1992), 'Social Change and Feminism: Three Generations of Women, Feminist Issues and the Women's Movement', unpublished Ph.D. thesis, University of Wales.

—— (1994a), 'Mannheim's Sociology of Generations: An Undervalued Legacy', *British Journal of Sociology*, 45: 481–95.

—— (1994b), 'Who Should Do the Dishes? Three Generations of Welsh Women Talking about Men and Housework', in J. Aaron *et al.* (eds.), *Our Sisters' Land: The Changing Identities of Women in Wales*, Cardiff: University of Wales Press.

—— DELAMONT, S., POWELL, G., REES, T., and READ, M. (1989), 'Evaluating a Women's Careers Convention: Methods, Results and Implications', *Research Papers in Education*, 4: 57–76.

—— and WILLIAMSON, H. (1988), *A Guide to Young People's Experiences in a Changing Labour Market*, London: Youthaid.

POLLARD, A. (1987) (ed.), *Children and their Primary Schools*, London: Falmer.

POLLOCK, L. (1983), *Forgotten Children: Parent–Child Relations from 1500–1900*, Cambridge: Cambridge University Press.

POSTMAN, N. (1983), *The Disappearance of Childhood*, London: W. H. Allen.

PROUT, A., and JAMES, A. (1990), 'A New Paradigm for the Sociology of Childhood? Provenance, Promise and Problems', in A. James and A. Prout (eds.), *Constructing and Reconstructing Childhood*, London: Falmer.

QVORTROP, J. (1990), 'A Voice for Children in Statistical and Social Accounting: A Plea for Children's Right to be Heard', in A. James and A. Prout (eds.), *Constructing and Reconstructing Childhood*, London: Falmer.

RICHARDS, A. (1982), *Chisunga: A Girls' Initiation Ceremony among the Bemba of Zambia*, London: Tavistock.

References

RILEY, M. WHITE (1984), 'Preface', in D. Kertzer and J. Keith (eds.), *Age and Anthropological Theory*, London: Cornell University Press.

RITCHIE, O., and KOLLER, M. (1964), *Sociology of Childhood*, New York: Meredith.

ROBERTS, C., and LANG, K. (1985), 'Generations and Ideological Change: Some Observations', *Public Opinion Quarterly*, 49: 460–73.

ROEBUCK, J. (1978), 'When Does Old Age Begin? The Evolution of the English Definition', *Journal of Social History*, 12: 416–28.

ROHEIM, G. (1974), *Children of the Desert*, New York: Harper.

ROSENMAYR, L. (1982), 'Biography and Identity', in T. Hareven and K. Adams (eds.), *Ageing and Life Course Transitions*, London: Tavistock.

ROSOW, I. (1978), 'What is a Cohort and Why?', *Human Development*, 21: 65–75.

ROSZAK, T. (1970), *The Making of a Counter Culture*, London: Faber and Faber.

SANDERS, C. (1993), 'Report fills third age void', *The Times Higher Educational Supplement*, 23 Apr.

SCHILDKROUT, E. (1978), 'Age and Gender in Hausa Society: Socio-economic Roles of Children in Urban Kano', in J. La Fontaine (ed.), *Sex and Age as Principles of Social Differentiation*, London: Althone Press.

SCHULLER, T. (1987), 'Second Adolescence? The Transition from Paid Work', *Work, Employment and Society*, 1: 352–70.

SCHUMAN, H., and RIEGER, C. (1992), 'Historical Analogies, Generational Effects and Attitudes toward War', *American Sociological Review*, 57: 315–26.

—— and SCOTT, J. (1989), 'Generations and Collective Memories', *American Historical Review*, 54: 359–81.

SEARS, D. (1983), 'The Persistence of Early Political Predispositions: The Roles of Attitude Object and Life Stage', in L. Wheeler and P. Sharer (eds.), *Review of Personality and Social Psychology*, vol. iv, Beverley Hills, Calif.: Sage.

SHIPMAN, M. (1972), *Childhood: A Sociological Perspective*, Windsor: NFER.

SMART, B. (1990), 'On the Disorder of Things: Sociology, Postmodernity and the "End of the Social"', *Sociology*, 24: 397–416.

SONTAG, S. (1979), 'The Double Standard of Ageing', in V. Carver and P. Liddiard (eds.), *An Ageing Population*, New York: Holmes and Meier.

SPITZER, A. (1973), 'The Historical Problem of Generations', *American Historical Review*, 78: 1353–85.

STEWART, A., and Healy, J. (1989), 'Linking Individual Development and Social Changes', *American Psychologist*, 44(1): 30–42.

STRINATI, D. (1992), 'Postmodernism and Popular Culture', *Sociology Review*, 1 (4): 2–7.

THANE, P. (1978), 'Non-contributory Versus Insurance Pensions, 1878–1908', in P. Thane (ed.), *The Origins of British Social Policy*, London: Croom Helm.

—— (1989), 'Old Age: Burden or Benefit?', in H. Joshi (ed.), *The Changing Population of Britain*, Oxford: Basil Blackwell.

THOMPSON, E. P. (1967), 'Time, Work-discipline and Industrial Capitalism', *Past and Present*, 38: 56–97.

THOMPSON, P., ITZIN, C., and ABENDSTERN, M. (1991), *I Don't Feel Old: Understanding the Experience of Later Life*, Oxford: Oxford University Press.

—— (1992), '"I Don't Feel Old"', *Ageing and Society*, 12: 23–47.

References

TOWNSEND, P. (1986), 'Ageism and Social Policy', in C. Phillipson and A. Walker (eds.), *Ageing and Social Policy*, Aldershot: Gower.

TROLL, L. (1970), 'Issues in the Study of Generations', *Aging and Human Development*, 1: 78–89.

TURNER, B. (1989), 'Ageing, Status Politics and Sociological Theory', *British Journal of Sociology*, 40: 588–606.

VICTOR, C. (1987), *Old Age in Modern Society*, London: Croom Helm.

WAGG, S. (1988), 'Perishing Kids? The Sociology of Childhood', *Social Studies Review*, 3 (4): 126–31.

—— (1992), '"One I Made Earlier": Media, Popular Culture and the Politics of Childhood', in D. Strinati and S. Wagg (eds.), *Come on down? Popular Culture in Postwar Britain*, London: Routledge.

WALKER, A. (1990), 'Poverty and Inequality in Old Age', in J. Bond and P. Coleman (eds.), *Ageing and Society*, London: Sage.

—— and PHILLIPSON, C. (1986), 'Introduction', in C. Phillipson and A. Walker (eds.), *Ageing and Social Policy*, Aldershot: Gower.

WALLACE, C. (1987), *For Richer, for Poorer: Growing up in and out of Work*, London: Tavistock.

WENGER, G. CLARE (1984), *The Supportive Network: Coping With Old Age*, London: George Allen and Unwin.

—— (1994), 'Old Women in Rural Wales: Variations in Adaption', in J. Aaron *et al.* (eds.), *Our Sisters' Land: The Changing Identities of Women in Wales*, Cardiff: University of Wales Press.

WILLIAMS, G. (1980), 'Warriors No More: A Study of the American Indian Elderly', in C. Fry (ed.), *Aging in Culture and Society*, New York: Praeger.

WILLIAMS, R. (1990), *A Protestant Legacy: Attitudes to Death and Illness among Older Aberdonians*, Oxford: Oxford University Press.

WILLIS, P. (1977), *Learning to Labour*, Farnborough: Saxon House.

—— (1984), 'Youth Unemployment 2: Ways of Living', *New Society*, 68 (115): 13–15.

WINTOUR, P. (1993), 'Pension age for women to be 65', *Guardian*, 12 Apr.

WITHERSPOON, S. (1985), 'Sex Roles and Gender Issues', in R. Jowell and S. Witherspoon (eds.), *British Social Attitudes*, Aldershot: Gower.

WRIGHT, R. (1991), 'Cohort Size and Earnings in Great Britain', *Journal of Population Economics*, 4: 295–305.

Index

Index

Index

Index

workending 94–5
Wright 137

youth:
  broken transitions 76
  chronological markers 58, 62, 72, 80
  coping strategies 70
  cross-cultural 65–6
  culture 66–70, 117, 139
  education 74
  employment 71, 72, 75, 76, 80
  ethnicity 61–2, 67, 70
  extension of 79

  family formation 72, 76, 78, 83
  and gender 64, 65–6, 67, 69, 70, 78
  history 63–5, 120–1, 146
  independence in 61
  modern Britain 60–3, 66–80
  physiological aspects 60–1
  school to employment transition 71, 76, 78
  and social class 64, 67, 69–70, 78
  sociological perspective on 80
  training schemes 74–5
  as transition 58, 73, 76, 78
  unemployment 72–3, 74